COACHING
&
MENTORING
FIRST-YEAR AND
STUDENT TEACHERS
SECOND EDITION

India J. Podsen
Vicki M. Denmark

Routledge
Taylor & Francis Group

LONDON AND NEW YORK

First published 2007 by Eye on Education

Published 2013 by Routledge
2 Park Square, Milton Park, Abingdon, Oxon OX14 4RN
711 Third Avenue, New York, NY, 10017, USA

Routledge is an imprint of the Taylor & Francis Group, an informa business

Library of Congress Cataloging-in-Publication Data
Podsen, India, 1945-
    Coaching and mentoring first-year and student teachers / India J. Podsen, Vicki M. Denmark. — 2nd ed.
        p. cm.
    ISBN 1-59667-039-8
1. Mentoring in education—United States. 2. Student teachers—United States. 3. First year teachers—United States. I.
Denmark, Vicki M., 1957-II. Title.
    LB1731.4.P63 2006
    370.71—dc22

                                                                                        2006030197

ISBN 13: 978-1-596-67039-6 (pbk)

Cover design & art by Carolyn H. Edlund Editorial, design
Production services provided by Freelance Editorial Services

Also Available from EYE ON EDUCATION

101 Answers for New Teachers and Their Mentors:
Effective Teaching Tips for Daily Classroom Use
Annette L. Breaux

What Great Teachers Do Differently:
14 Things That Matter Most
Todd Whitaker

Classroom Motivation From A to Z:
How To Engage Your Students in Learning
Barbara R. Blackburn

REAL Teachers, REAL Challenges, REAL Solutions:
25 Ways to Handle the Challenges of the Classroom Effectively
Annette and Elizabeth Breaux

Classroom Management Simplified!
Elizabeth Breaux

How to Reach and Teach ALL Students— Simplified!
Elizabeth Breaux

Teach Me—I Dare You!
Brough, Bergman, and Holt

Great Quotes for Great Educators
Todd Whitaker and Dale Lumpa

Handbook on Differentiated Instruction
for Middle and High Schools
Sheryn Spencer Northey

Best Practices to Help At-Risk Learners
Franklin P. Schargel

Active Literacy Across the Curriculum:
Strategies for Reading, Writing, Speaking and Listening
Heidi Hayes Jacobs

Differentiated Instruction:
A Guide for Elementary School Teachers
Amy Benjamin

MEET THE AUTHORS

India J. Podsen, a former teacher and middle school administrator, is Professor of Middle/Secondary Education and Coordinator of the Education Specialist Program in Teacher Leadership and the Educational Leadership Endorsement at North Georgia College and State University. Both programs were awarded national recognition by the Educational Leaders Constituent Council (ELCC) in 2005. Formerly, the director of the Principals Center at Georgia State University, she is the author of numerous articles and books. Dr. Podsen has collaborated with schools to design effective teacher induction and mentoring programs.

Vicki M. Denmark, a former classroom teacher, middle school principal, and university professor, currently serves as an Area Superintendent with the Fulton County School system in Atlanta, Georgia. She has served on the Executive Board for the Georgia Middle Schools Association and was the president of the organization for two years. Currently, she serves on the Executive Board for the Georgia Lighthouse Schools to Watch program and as the Southern Regional Trustee for the National Middle School Association. She continues to teach as an adjunct professor in the area of Educational Policy Studies and works closely with the schools on mentoring and supervising first year teachers and administrators.

TABLE OF CONTENTS

COACHING & MENTORING ACTIVITIES

1

SINK OR SWIM—
YOU'RE ON YOUR OWN

SCENARIO ONE

Lori Adams was honored when her principal asked her to serve as a cooperating teacher for a student intern from Gateway College. She knew her principal considered her to be a very effective eighth grade math teacher and her annual performance evaluations supported this endorsement. After 10 years of teaching both middle and high school students, Lori was eager to share her expertise with an aspiring teacher. The intern would be with her for four weeks from 7:45 a.m. until noon, completing the required extended field experience just before student teaching for a full semester.

Lori's first week with Christy Johnson dampened her enthusiasm. Although she had oriented Christy to the school, her class procedures, and her expectations, the student intern seemed unresponsive and very unsure of herself. Lori thought this attitude was due to lack of experience and fear of the unknown. She smiled to herself, remembering how intimidating her first year of teaching had been, but she had gotten through it. In Lori's mind, it was a sink or swim proposition. The first week passed with Christy observing Lori's teaching style, reflecting daily in her teaching log about what she observed, getting to know the students, and meeting with her college supervisor. Christy gave Lori a copy of her four-week extended teaching guide outlining her field requirements, suggested tips and observation forms for mentor teachers, and a projected timeline for class visitations and conferences.

During the second week, Lori asked Christy to prepare her required seven-day teaching unit. Lori picked her second period math class because she knew that the students would provide many opportunities for Christy to demonstrate her classroom management skills. "She might as well face the music from the very beginning," Lori mused. Christy presented her plans, drafting them as she had been taught in her teacher preparation program. Lori looked them over and commented, "These are very detailed, but you won't have enough time to do this for every class. But I guess you have to do them this way for your college supervisor. What do they know?" Lori laughed, but Christy just shrugged her shoulders. The second week concluded with Christy shadowing a student for a day, observing the team planning meetings, and developing materials for her math unit. The college supervisor set up a meeting time with Christy and her mentor teacher, but Lori canceled it at the last minute because of an urgent parent conference.

Christy stood before the second period class and started her unit during the third week. Lori sat in the back of the class and observed. The intern conducted the lesson in a satisfactory way and managed the class better than she expected. After introducing the objective and relating it to the students' life experiences, Christy presented a concise 20-minute lecture on the math concept and then followed it up with practice examples, which the students completed in teams of two. She walked around the room using proximity to keep students on task. At one point, Christy moved in on a student who was passing notes and spoke quietly to her. She responded by putting the note in her book bag. At the conclusion of the lesson, Christy summarized the concepts, assigned homework, and dismissed the class.

Before the next class arrived, Lori turned to Christy and commented, "Good job, but you didn't do enough checking for understanding and guided practice before letting them work in teams. I usually don't put these students in any groups because they are so chatty. I suggest you do the same." Christy started to ask a question, but Lori moved to the door to greet the entering students, saying, "We'll discuss this lesson later." But later never came. Planning time was consumed with team meetings, parent conferences, and the endless stream of paperwork that came with the job.

By the end of the fourth week, Lori was glad to see Christy go. They had never developed the kind of rapport that Lori anticipated. The intern's questions seemed to challenge her way of teaching and often Christy did not respond to her suggestions. How could she help Christy if she didn't take her advice! Lori completed the required field experience assessment form rating Christy as having "good" potential to be a teacher. Being a cooperating teacher just wasn't what she expected.

Scenario Two

William Fox had mixed feelings when the principal assigned him to be a teacher buddy for a first-year teacher at Kingston High School. He had just completed his fifth year of teaching math and expected to finish his masters at a nearby university within the next semester. He wondered why the principal had asked him to take on this assignment and hoped it wouldn't require any after school demands on his time.

The principal held a brief orientation for the seven first-year teachers and their assigned teaching buddies. William concluded that the meeting was more an overview of school rules and procedures rather than a chance to clarify the expectations of the buddy system that had materialized over the summer break. The orientation session ended with about 10 minutes for the new teachers and their buddies to socialize and get to know one another a little better. William looked into the face of Tom Sparks, who smiled warmly and expressed his eagerness to teach by saying, "I've had a terrific student teaching experience and can't wait to have a class of my own." They chatted casually and William encouraged Tom to call on him when he had questions or if he needed any help.

Two weeks passed and William had not heard from Tom. He concluded no news was probably good news. Not wanting to appear intrusive or interfering, William left a brief note in Tom's box conveying the notion that he hoped things were going well and to call if he wanted to talk about any problems or concerns. Tom replied by asking where he could get certain supplies and what the procedure was to fill out various administrative forms that he recently received. William promptly responded and made a copy of the forms he completed so Tom would have an example. William dropped by Tom's classroom, located in one of the outside trailers, to personally hand him the forms. He thought the young teacher looked a bit glum as Tom sat quietly at his desk during his planning period; the quick, eager smile did not come forth as William greeted the first-year teacher and inquired how things were going.

William looked around the drab walls and remembered how alone he had felt when he had started his first year of teaching. He tried to cheer his young colleague by telling him he also started out in a trailer but eventually worked his way into the main building. Tom responded with a half-hearted smile. William asked about his classes and soon learned that Tom had four different course preparations for his five classes and a quick glance at his class rosters told him Tom had at least two classes that had become "dumping grounds" for students with chronic behavior problems and learning difficulties. Yes, William thought, the rites of passage into the teaching profession could be hazardous, and trial and error seemed to be embedded in the process.

As the semester moved along with fall fading into winter, William ran into Tom at faculty meetings, or coming or going in the parking lot. Their interactions were friendly and focused more on general topics and sports. After the semester break, William returned to school to find a note in his box from the principal. Tom had turned in his resignation during the winter holiday break and would not be back. Tom told the principal that teaching was just not what he expected and that he just didn't feel capable of doing the job well. He decided to leave teaching and find another career. William was surprised that Tom had quit. What had happened to the bright-eyed young teacher who wanted to teach kids?

TOUGHING IT OUT

Whether you are mentoring a student intern or a first-year teacher, Debra Pitton (1998) tells us that "dealing with problems in education is never easy. There are seldom clear-cut solutions." She points out simply that there are multiple factors surrounding the complex situation of teaching and, of course, there are multiple perspectives about how it all should be done. We know quite often that pedagogy is the main focus in our teacher preparation programs, but once out in the field, student interns must also confront a roller coaster ride of emotions and personalities within the context of the school community. Likewise, entry-level teachers face the realities of surviving the first year in the profession but, unlike student interns, often have no assistance and are fearful of asking for help. Stephen Gordon (1991) comments that "despite good intentions and high expectations of these beginners, 40 to 50 percent of them will drop out of teaching within the first seven years, most within the first two years." He concludes that those who manage to get through the first year have such disappointing experiences that "many never reach their full potential as educators."

Similarly, cooperating teacher and peer mentors are also left to tough it out without any training for the sensitive and supportive role they have willingly embraced and expected to demonstrate. Both teacher mentors and their mentees need to be aware of the relationship that should develop within practicum and first-year experiences, as well as the anxiety these interactions can produce.

STUDENT INTERNSHIPS AND ENTRY-LEVEL REALITIES

Field experiences, whether they are short weekly observation visits or extended field visitations, provide snapshots of actual schools with real children and teachers. For some aspiring teachers, it's the place where the "rubber meets the road"; it's the first chance for interns to determine whether they really like teaching with all its special challenges. In each field situation, teacher interns enter classrooms belonging to other professionals—a person like you, whom they usually don't know and who may demonstrate a teaching style or classroom management approach that differs from their own scheme of how things ought to be.

They find themselves in unfamiliar territory faced with two taskmasters—you, the cooperating teacher, and their college supervisor (Bullough & Draper, 2004). Even under the best circumstances, student interns constantly question their ability to successfully complete the experience, asking such questions as: "How can I make my cooperating teacher happy? What am I expected to do? Will I get a good recommendation from my mentor teacher? How can I get all of my coursework done and still plan and teach lessons? Is my college supervisor satisfied with my progress? What happens if I don't do well? Will I still be able to graduate?" Depending on the intern's confidence level and current skills, and the consistency among the taskmasters, these questions get answered or they multiply.

For beginning teachers, the enormous responsibility of the job finally hits home and this feeling is significantly overwhelming when things don't go as planned. Gordon (1991) gives us five environmental factors that confront novice teachers:

1. Difficult Work Assignments	Often beginning teachers start the job with larger classes, more difficult students, and more course preparations than experienced teachers.

2. Unclear Expectations	In addition to the formal expectations cited in faculty handbooks, there are a myriad of informal routines and customs that make up the school culture.
3. Inadequate Resources	First-year teachers lack the stockpile of years of instructional materials and often their classrooms have been stripped of better furniture, materials, and equipment.
4. Isolation	Many entry-level teachers view seeking help as an admission of incompetence and continually hide serious problems.
5. Reality Shock	The discrepancy between the novice teacher's vision of teaching and the job realities of the situation can cause serious depression, which tends to impact the other factors and make them even more unbearable.

Each of these factors brings its own set of problems, which are intensified when experienced teachers avoid helping new teachers, believing that it's not their job or that their advice would be viewed as meddling. With new teacher attrition rates of 15 percent and higher for each of the first few years, it seems logical to develop an assistance program to address these issues, especially because it's the most promising teachers who exit the profession (Gordon, 1991, p. 7). Furthermore, Gordon tells us that those teachers who make it through the first three years often develop a "survival mentality" that negatively impacts on their openness to be reflective and highly skilled teachers.

A VIABLE OPTION

And so this dilemma brings us to you. There never seems to be enough time in any teacher-preparation or mentoring program to help interns and first-year colleagues develop the teaching and classroom management skills that they need. The pressure on them is great. We know cooperating teacher and first-year mentors also feel this same pressure: the pressure to be successful with an inexperienced intern or colleague. We admit that you are frequently left on your own with this awesome responsibility to help an intern or beginner make major strides in a very short period of time. This book will help you become a capable cooperating teacher and peer mentor. The topics in this book will answer your questions and address your concerns as you assist an intern or entry-level teacher in becoming a competent professional.

HOW TO USE THIS GUIDE

TO THE COOPERATING TEACHER AND FIRST-YEAR PEER MENTOR

This book is a resource tool that has been designed as a way for you to develop your knowledge and skills as a mentor for an aspiring teacher or a first-year colleague. Its purpose is threefold:

- ♦ To help you assess what you need to know about effective performance coaching and career mentoring.

- ♦ To enhance your knowledge and skills as it relates to the successful components in effective mentoring programs.

- ♦ To provide hands-on coaching and mentoring strategies and tools to assist you in the teacher-mentoring process.

We begin Part I: Preparation for Mentor Training with exercises that focus on your current attitudes and behaviors toward teacher mentoring on the job. This analysis sets the stage for the information provided in the eight critical skill modules that every co-operating teacher and first-year peer mentor need to know about and the coaching tools that will make your job easier and more professionally rewarding.

In Part Two: Competency Training Modules, we present the key factors that teacher mentors encounter in the coaching process. We took the "what you need to know approach" in each component. Each training module presents all or a combination of these elements:

- ♦ Essential information on a particular aspect of the mentoring role.

- ♦ Exercises to reinforce the concepts presented.

- ♦ Mentoring strategies to use with interns and first-year teachers on the job.

- ♦ Coaching boosters to help you synthesize and reflect on the concepts more in depth.

TO THE STAFF DEVELOPER OR COLLEGE INSTRUCTOR

This book fosters successful mentoring relationships in schools by providing ongoing assistance to student interns or new teachers. If you are a staff developer or school administrator responsible for new teacher induction and mentoring in your district or school, the training modules can stand alone and be used to develop short in-service workshops targeted at training teacher mentors in your workplace.

If you are an instructor in a teacher preparation program responsible for field observations or a coordinator for student teaching placement, the text provides helpful information on what is expected of cooperating teachers. A review of the competency modules during orientation sessions for cooperating teachers will outline an action plan to guide cooperating teachers through the important tasks that they have willingly embraced but in which they have no formal training to help point the way.

Each module is focused on a particular aspect of the mentoring process. Cooperating teachers and first-year peer mentors can self-assess their knowledge and skills and then go directly to a particular module for specific information and skill building. In this way, veteran teachers continue their professional growth as instructional experts while strengthening their ability as teacher mentors. The appendix provides additional coaching and mentoring instruments.

REFERENCES

Bullough, R.V., & R.J. Draper. (2004). Making sense of a failed triad: Mentors, university supervisors, and positioning theory. *Journal of Teacher Education*, 55 (5), 407–420.

Gordon, S. P. (1991). *How to help beginning teachers succeed*. Alexandria, VA: Association for Supervision and Curriculum Development.

Pitton, D. E. (1998). *Stories of student teaching: A case approach to the student teaching experience*. Upper Saddle River, NJ: Merrill/Prentice Hall.

COACHING BOOSTERS

Boreen, J., & D. Niday. (2003). *Mentoring across boundaries: Helping beginning teachers succeed in challenging situations*. Portland, MA: Stenhouse Publishers.

Boyer, L., & P. Gillespie. (2000). Keeping the committed: The importance of induction and support programs for new special educators. *Teaching Exceptional Children*, 33 (6), 10–15.

Gratch, A. (1998). Beginning teacher and mentoring relationships. *Journal of Teacher Education*, 49, 220–227.

Johnson, S., & S. Kardos. (2005). Bridging the generation gap. *Educational Leadership*, 62 (8), 8–14.

_____ (1999). *Mentoring to Improve Schools*. Association for Supervision and Curriculum Development. Videotape Series. Stock #499323J17.

2

FROM MASTER TEACHER TO MASTERFUL MENTOR

Congratulations! Because you are reading this book, chances are that you have been selected to be a cooperating teacher for a preservice intern or peer mentor for a beginning teacher. We can't stress enough the importance of your role in navigating this aspiring professional through the murky waters ahead. You have been chosen because you represent the "best of the best." However, being a master teacher doesn't always prepare you to be a masterful mentor. Unlike our colleagues Lori and William (see Scenario One, p. i, and Scenario Two, p. ii, in the Introduction), we want your coaching and mentoring experience to be highly successful for your mentee and professionally rewarding for you. This text is centered on assisting cooperating teachers who work with student interns and peer mentors who work with first-year teachers.

WHY WE NEED YOU, THE MASTER TEACHER

Mentoring is a critical topic in education today and a favored strategy in U.S. policy initiatives that are focused on teacher induction (Feiman-Nemser, 1993). Besides creating new career opportunities for veteran teachers, coaching and mentoring novices provides a quantum leap over the abrupt and unassisted entry into teaching that characterizes the experience of many beginners. You may have decided to be a cooperating teacher or first-year peer mentor because your transition into the teaching profession was less than ideal and because you wanted to change that process. But whatever your reason, your role in the teacher-induction phase is crucial.

According to Ingersoll & Smith (2003), nearly 40 to 50 percent of all beginning teachers leave the profession within the first five years of their career and cite job dissatisfaction as a major reason. Research indicates that the most creative and talented new educators are often the most likely to exit our profession (Gonzales & Sosa, 1993). Why are we losing the brightest and best young professionals? As professional educators, we must reflect on our role in helping novices do more than just survive during their critical entry into the teaching profession. With nearly two million new teachers targeted to enter U.S. schools in the next decade, the challenge of supporting them through extended field experiences and their first year of teaching is a critical issue for both teacher-education programs and school districts. Linda Darling Hammond, executive director of the National Commission on Teaching and America's Future, asserts, "To retain new teachers, we must do two things: design good schools in which to teach and employ mentoring" (Halford, 1998, p. 34).

SO WHAT IS MENTORING?

Mentoring can be defined as a sustained relationship between a novice and an expert. In a clearly defined teacher-mentoring relationship, the expert provides help, support, and guidance that helps the novice develop the necessary skills to enter or continue on his or her career path. As a mentor, you have two main roles, as an expert and as a role model, in your teaching field.

Now, here is the dilemma: Enthusiasm for mentoring has not been supported by a clearly defined purpose for mentoring and the training needed to support the mentors. Rowley (1999) tells us that many school districts have moved toward pairing veteran teachers with beginning teachers. He points out, however, that "this prevalent aspect of school-based mentoring programs presents special challenges which are further exacerbated when mentor teachers receive no or inadequate training and only token support for their work" (p. 20). Moreover, the educational community understands that mentors can have a positive effect on novices, but there is a big gap in deciding what mentors should do, what they actually do, and what novices should learn as a result. The research on student teaching highlights the conservative influence of cooperating teachers and school cultures on novices' practice (Feiman-Nemser, Parker, & Zeichner, 1993). More specifically, this research confirms that most cooperating teachers promote conventional norms and practices rather than modeling continual reforms of effective practices within their own classrooms and schools (Cochran-Smith, 1991).

Cooperating teachers and peer mentors have little experience with the key activities associated with the mentoring process—observing, discussing, and providing specific feedback on performance. When was the last time you observed a colleague or had a colleague observe you? How often do you analyze what you do well and target what you could do better? When was the last time you discussed your teaching performance with a peer? What we refer to is the type of assistance that is separate from the formal evaluation process.

Most teachers work single-handedly, in the privacy of their classrooms, protected by conventions of self-governance and noninterference. The culture of teaching does not encourage distinctions among teachers based on expertise. Little (1990) concludes that the persistence of privacy, the omission of peer coaching and reflection within the school culture, and the tendency of school administrators to treat all teachers the same limits what you can do. Because you have not had the chance to practice the essential skills of mentoring, you may find the role of coach and mentor a bit frustrating. In addition, your current teaching practices may or may not match the learner-centered teaching advocated by most teacher-education programs. Are you willing to develop the collaborative contexts where mentors and mentees can explore their teaching styles together and be flexible with both traditional and new ways of thinking and acting associated with effective teaching practice? (Jonson, 2002; Wasley, 1999; Rowley, 1999)

SUMMARY

*"A total commitment is paramount to reaching the
ultimate in performance."*

Tom Flores, NFL Coach,
NASSP, 1985

This guide will help you make mentoring meaningful. In an ideal world, this would consist of specialized professional development consisting of coursework, district support, tangible incentives, and release time. In a less than ideal world, this guide provides tools that will enable you to understand and apply the skills essential to being a masterful mentor.

REFERENCES

Cochran-Smith, M. (1991). Learning to teach against the grain. *Harvard Educational Review, 61*(3), 279–310.

Feiman-Nemser, S. (1993). *Teacher mentoring: A critical review.* ERIC Clearinghouse on Teaching and Teacher Education (http://www.ericsp.org/95-2.html).

Feiman-Nemser, S., M. B. Parker, & K. Zeichner. (1993). Are mentor teachers teacher educators? In D. McIntyre, H. Hagger, & M. Wilkin (eds), *Mentoring: Perspectives on school-based teacher educators* (pp. 147–165). London: Kogan Page.

Gonzales, F., & A. S. Sosa. (March 1993). How do we keep teachers in our classrooms? The TNT response. *IDRA Newsletter,* 1, 6–9.

Halford, J. (1998). Easing the way for new teachers. *Educational Leadership, 55*(5), 33–36.

Ingersoll, R.M., & T.M. Smith. (2004). The wrong solution to the teacher shortage. *Educational Leadership*, 60(8), 30–33.

Jonson, K. (2002). *Being an effective mentor: How to help beginning teachers succeed.* Thousand Oaks, CA: Corwin Press Inc.

Little, J. W. (1990). The mentoring phenomenon and the social organization of teaching. In C. Cazden (ed), *Review of research in education.* Vol. 16 (pp. 297–351). Washington, DC: American Educational Research Association.

Rowley, J. (1999). The good mentor, *Educational Leadership,* 56(8), 20–22.

Wasley, P. (1999). Teaching worth celebrating, *Educational Leadership,* 56(8), 8–13.

COACHING BOOSTERS

Induction approaches. *The New Teacher Center at the University of California at Santa Cruz.* Retrieved June 1, 2006, from http://www.newteachercenter.org

Standards for quality and effectiveness for professional teacher induction programs. *Beginning Teacher Support and Assessment Program.* Retrieved June 1, 2006, from http://www.bsta.ca.gov

Stansbury, K., & J. Zimmerman. (2002). Smart induction programs become lifelines for the beginning teacher. *Journal of Staff Development*, Fall 2002, 10–17.

Useem, E., & R. C, Neild. (2005). Supporting new teachers in the city, *Educational Leadership*, 62(8), 36–39.

Wayne, A., Youngs, P., & S. Fleischman. (2005). Improving teacher induction. *Educational Leadership*, 62(8), 76–77.

3

ASSESSING YOUR COACHING AND MENTORING APTITUDE

As a master teacher, you have developed a vast repertoire of personal and technical tools for dealing with classroom teaching and behavior management. You have successfully designed thousands of routines and procedures for handling the day-to-day problems of working with more than 100 students, teammates, and parents.

On top of all of this, you are taking on the responsibility of guiding a neophyte into the profession. Master teachers who have current information about effective coaching and mentoring competencies are far more likely to develop a collaborative and systematic plan in reaching their goal. In this chapter, you will determine your own areas of strength as they pertain to your role of mentor. The results of your analysis will enable you to set specific learning goals as you begin your journey from master teacher to masterful mentor.

EXERCISE A. THE MENTOR'S APTITUDE INVENTORY

Let's examine your aptitude about the notion of coaching and mentoring. Below are a series of statements. There are no right or wrong answers to these statements. Indicate the degree to which each statement applies to you by checking the appropriate box. Take your time and try to be as honest as possible.

1. Very little knowledge and skill.
2. Some knowledge and skill.
3. Adequate knowledge and skill.
4. Better than adequate knowledge and skill.
5. Quite knowledgeable and very skillful.

COMPETENCY 1: UNDERSTANDING THE MENTORING ROLE

MY TOTAL = _____

	Skill Statement	1	2	3	4	5
1.	Know how mentoring is defined, described, or explained within the context of teacher induction.					
2.	Know the mentor role, tasks, and responsibilities.					
3.	Know the key components to effective teacher induction programs.					
4.	Identify how mentors are selected and trained.					
5.	Know the qualifications of an effective mentor teacher.					
6.	Identify problems or issues related to mentoring novice teachers.					
7.	Select or create and apply an instrument by which you can diagnosis mentee performance.					
8.	Select or create and apply an instrument by which you can assess your performance as a mentor.					
9.	Identify the benefits of teacher mentoring for experienced teachers, novices, and the school community.					
	Total the Xs in each column and multiply by the number at the top. Place the subtotal for each column in the shaded box and then add the scores across each column for the Total. Highest total for this competency is 45 and the lowest is 9. Place your total above.					

COMPETENCY 2: PROMOTING COLLABORATIVE LEARNING

MY TOTAL = _____

	Skill Statement	1	2	3	4	5
1.	Demonstrate the ability to establish rapport and build trust with novices.					
2.	Demonstrate the ability to develop collaboratively both short- and long-term performance goals.					
3.	Demonstrate the ability to plan and implement an action plan to address performance goals.					
4.	Demonstrate and model effective conflict resolution skills and approaches.					
5.	Demonstrate the ability to provide constructive criticism without appearing judgmental.					
6.	Apply a problem-solving approach in dealing with conflict or performance issues that may arise.					
7.	Identify, select, and apply performance criteria reflective of effective teaching.					
8.	Establish a process for observation and systematic feedback.					
9.	Develop a plan to involve teaching peers in designing a best team experience for novices.					
	Total the Xs in each column and multiply by the number at the top. Place the subtotal for each column in the shaded box and then add the scores across each column for the Total. Highest total for this competency is 45 and the lowest is 9. Place your total above.					

COMPETENCY 3:
NURTURING THE NOVICE

MY TOTAL = _____

	Skill Statement	1	2	3	4	5
1.	Know how to sequence the teaching tasks to build both knowledge and skills.					
2.	Understand and apply sound principles of adult learning.					
3.	Provide emotional support during times of personal or career stress and guidance for decision making.					
4.	Understand the importance of socializing the intern within the contexts of the profession and the school community.					
5.	Know the key tasks related to successful cognitive coaching.					
6.	Increase your skill in conducting high level thinking conversations with novices and peers about their teaching.					
7.	Know the major aspects of the novice's teacher preparation program in order to build on previous learning.					
8.	Know how to help novices diagnosis needs in order to target constructive feedback.					
	Total the Xs in each column and multiply by the number at the top. Place the subtotal for each column in the shaded box and then add the scores across each column for the Total. Highest total for this competency is 40 and the lowest is 8. Place your total above.					

COMPETENCY 4: DEVELOPING YOUR PERFORMANCE-COACHING SKILLS

MY TOTAL = _____

	Skill Statement	1	2	3	4	5
1.	Identify the steps involved in performance coaching.					
2.	Know the basic sequence of courses and experiences novices take within their preparation programs.					
3.	Demonstrate the ability to co-teach or team teacher with novices and understand its importance.					
4.	Develop the skills of observing and collecting specific, descriptive data about performance of novices.					
5.	Know how to sequence teaching tasks based on the conceptual level of novices.					
6.	Know the key characteristics of effective feedback.					
7.	Know the five phases of clinical supervision and their purposes.					
8.	Demonstrate the ability to implement each phase of the clinical/coaching cycle.					
9.	Know and understand how novices' levels of abstract thinking might impact on performance.					
10.	Demonstrate the ability to develop postobservation conferences based on performance and level of conceptual thinking.					
	Total the Xs in each column and multiply by the number at the top. Place the subtotal for each column in the shaded box and then add the scores across each column for the Total. Highest total for this competency is 50 and the lowest is 10. Place your total above.					

COMPETENCY 5:
MODELING AND COACHING
EFFECTIVE TEACHING STANDARDS

MY TOTAL = _____

	Skill Statement	1	2	3	4	5
1.	Know the components of successful teacher mentoring.					
2.	Understand contemporary views of teaching and learning.					
3.	Know local, state, and national standards for effective teaching.					
4.	Demonstrate the ability to model successful instructional behaviors linked to a framework of effective practice.					
5.	Demonstrate the ability to sequence instructional behaviors from simple to complex.					
6.	Know current standards and strategies for assessing and monitoring student learning.					
7.	Apply performance and cognitive coaching skills in order to help novices translate content knowledge and pedagogical skills into successful instructional behaviors.					
	Total the Xs in each column and multiply by the number at the top. Place the subtotal for each column in the shaded box and then add the scores across each column for the Total. Highest total for this competency is 35 and the lowest is 7. Place your total above.					

COMPETENCY 6: MODELING AND COACHING EFFECTIVE CLASSROOM MANAGEMENT STANDARDS

MY TOTAL = _____

	Skill Statement	*1*	*2*	*3*	*4*	*5*
1.	Understand the major classroom principles associated with effective practice in managing the classroom.					
2.	Establish classroom rules and procedures and model their implementation.					
3.	Create a positive, businesslike learning climate based on self-discipline and motivation.					
4.	Know the relationship between classroom management and instruction.					
5.	Understand the impact of diversity in the classroom as it relates to managing student behavior.					
6.	Demonstrate the ability to apply interventions systematically and understand their consequences.					
7.	Demonstrate the ability to deal effectively with both off-task and disruptive behavior problems.					
	Total the Xs in each column and multiply by the number at the top. Place the subtotal for each column in the shaded box and then add the scores across each column for the Total. Highest total for this competency is 35 and the lowest is 7. Place your total above.					

COMPETENCY 7:
DISPLAYING SENSITIVITY TO
INDIVIDUAL DIFFERENCES

MY TOTAL = _____

	Skill Statement	1	2	3	4	5
1.	Understand the importance of helping all learners reach high levels of achievement.					
2.	Know about race, gender, class, and cultural diversity and its implications in the classroom.					
3.	Understand learning styles and how learning preferences impact the ways that students respond to teaching and learning.					
4.	Know the impact pact of educational policy (i.e., Public Law 94-142 and No Child Left Behind) on teaching and learning for all students.					
5.	Demonstrate how to capitalize on cultural diversity by modeling culturally responsive teaching behaviors.					
6.	Know the impact of poverty on student learning and achievement.					
7.	Understand the factors associated with at-risk students and show ways to reach and teach these students.					
	Total the Xs in each column and multiply by the number at the top. Place the subtotal for each column in the shaded box and then add the scores across each column for the Total. Highest total for this competency is 35 and the lowest is 7. **Place your total above.**					

COMPETENCY 8: SHAPING PROFESSIONAL RELATIONSHIPS

MY TOTAL = _____

	Skill Statement	1	2	3	4	5
1.	Understand the changing role of teachers in a standards-based world.					
2.	Know and articulate the value of being a teacher-leader within the educational community.					
3.	Understand the National Board for Professional Teaching Standards as they impact the teaching profession.					
4.	Demonstrate the ability to show professional contributions to the school, district, and the profession.					
5.	Know the indicators for determining competency in the area of professional responsibilities.					
6.	Apply performance-coaching skills in assisting novices to manage all aspects of the teaching role.					
	Total the Xs in each column and multiply by the number at the top. Place the subtotal for each column in the shaded box and then add the scores across each column for the Total. Highest total for this competency is 30 and the lowest is 6. **Place your total above.**					

EXERCISE B. ANALYZING YOUR MENTORING KNOWLEDGE AND SKILLS

Return to each section and add up your score for each competency module. Now record it on the chart below. In what competency areas are your strengths? What areas need work? Once you have analyzed your responses, outline an action plan for investigating competency areas that interest you most or that reveal that you need more information and skill.

SUMMARY ANALYSIS

	Competency Area	Highest Score Possible	Your Total	Strength or Growth Target
1.	Understanding the Mentoring Role	45		
2.	Promoting Collaborative Learning	45		
3.	Nurturing the Novice	40		
4.	Developing Your Performance Coaching Skills	50		
5.	Modeling and Coaching Effective Teaching Standards	35		
6.	Modeling and Coaching Effective Classroom Management Standards	35		
7.	Displaying Sensitivity to Individual Differences	35		
8.	Shaping Professional Relationships	30		
	Grand Total	315	*Your Total*	

4

SIZING UP THE
SITUATION

CASE STUDY

Your principal announces that your school, a recent winner of the National School of Excellence Award, has been invited to collaborate with the local university in the preparation and support of both preservice interns and first-year teachers. In particular, the university is seeking schools to participate as partners in developing Professional Development Schools as a way of involving master teachers in the training and development of teachers.

Your principal informs you that recent reforms in teacher education are moving away from just reading and talking about pedagogy to methods that provide opportunities for novices, university instructors, and experienced K-12 teachers to observe, practice, and reflect collaboratively both within college classrooms and within schools. To accomplish this goal, the university's teacher-education faculty desires to link college classrooms with K-12 classrooms by developing ongoing conversations between college instructors and practitioners, and partnerships between the Schools of Education and local school districts.

EXERCISE C. YOUR VIEWS ON TEACHER PREPARATION

Your principal wants to know how you stand on this proposal and what questions you have about being involved as a cooperating teacher or first-year peer mentor. Jot down your ideas and questions.

Cooperating Teacher Mentor	*First-Year Peer Mentor*
What were your needs as a student teacher?	Think about your first year in the classroom. What went well and what could have made it better for you?
How were they met?	
	Did you have an assigned buddy?
Describe the qualities of your supervising teacher?	
	If you did, how did a peer buddy assist you?
How would you describe your field experiences?	What ideas and suggestions do you have about mentoring a first-year teacher?
How many did you have? What would have made them better?	
What ideas do you have about coaching student interns?	What questions and concerns do you have about being a peer mentor?
What concerns do you have?	

RECENT TRENDS IN TEACHER EDUCATION

The expression, "You've come a long way baby," may best describe how we feel about the advancements that have been made in trying to bring some semblance of order and collegiality to the complexity of becoming a teacher. "Concerns about too little training and lack of follow-through for beginning teachers have led teacher-education institutions and cooperating schools to revamp their teaching programs" (Scherer, 1998, p. 5). Let's see how close we come to answering some of your questions.

What were your needs as a teacher trainee? Probably your biggest need was confronting the fear of the unknown and the fear of failure. There you are in your senior year after three years of feeling fairly successful learning your content. Now your student-teaching requirement thrusts you into a real classroom with a real teacher and at least 30 moving bodies who call you Ms. or Mr.

Now what? You feel nervous and anxious because for first time you are being asked to perform multiple teaching tasks simultaneously, usually without the benefit of any practice and coaching on these tasks. Now, for the first time, you begin to realize how complex the job may be, what you can do well, and how much more you need to know. However, you've got to get through this because graduation is just ahead, your parents have already sent out the invitations, and you've got a teaching job offer lined up. Nothing like adding a little more pressure to perform to it all.

WHAT IS A PROFESSIONAL DEVELOPMENT SCHOOL AND WHY DO WE NEED THEM?

Think about your first classroom and your students. How would you describe them now and how would you describe them when you first started teaching? Chances are you might say that you are being asked to teach a very diverse student body and to account for higher student achievement than ever before. Think about how you developed your expertise in your subject matter and your teaching style. Does trial and error come to mind? Or trial by fire! Chances are you didn't have many opportunities to practice or receive on-the-job coaching, reflect about successes and failures, or dialogue with a peer through well-planned mentorship experiences. Perhaps you didn't have any field experiences at all prior to student teaching. Chances are you managed to get through student teaching or your first year by the seat of your pants with or without the help of a well-meaning experienced teacher who gave it his or her best shot.

Traditional teacher-education training practices mean trying to find enough cooperating teachers from enough schools to take on the responsibility of supervising a novice. Generally, there is little systematic planning in matching novices to experts, checking out how or why experts are selected, or collaborating with cooperating teachers on how the experience might develop. In schools, beginning teachers may be assigned a buddy who shows the new teacher how to maneuver in the system and is available should the novice seek help. However, the buddy rarely visits the beginner's classroom, and after a few weeks the interactions become sporadic.

The notion of Professional Development Schools brings unique opportunities to bridge the gap between college and K-12 classrooms. In such partnerships, novices learn from a cadre of colleagues—including administrators, cooperating teachers, school specialists, counselors, their cohort group, and college instructors. In such settings, interns have the opportunity to observe, practice, and reflect on multiple perspectives and practices before they take on the responsibility of managing their own classes. In such settings, beginning teachers have skilled peer mentors who know the risks facing new teachers and help novices by minimizing these risks or eliminating them when possible, with administrative support. Here are some practices associated with the Professional Development School (PDS) concept:

♦ College instructors collaborate with administrators and teachers in selecting and assigning preservice interns to particular teachers.

♦ Cooperating teachers, interns, and college instructors discuss what a new intern must know and be able to do at different stages of career growth.

♦ Regular debriefing conferences are held between and among all stakeholders, not only to critique performance but also to discuss problems and strategies to resolve them.

◆ When effective collegial partnerships are formed between novices and teacher mentors, preservice interns remain at PDS to continue their career development into student teaching or first-year teaching.

◆ College professors develop ongoing working relationships with K-12 practitioners and become connected to current school curriculums, teaching practices, classroom management techniques, and students in today's schools.

◆ Both university and school faculty plan and teach interns in these programs. Master teachers serve as adjunct faculty, coaches, mentors, and teacher leaders, thus expanding their knowledge and skill base.

◆ In PDS both novices and mentor teachers have collegial help and resources on site. University personnel have the opportunity to interact with both student interns and first-year teachers to assess the quality of teacher-education preparation and to use these data to improve programs.

To summarize, the professional development school is just one way teacher-education programs and interested school systems are trying to improve teaching training and the retention of first-year teachers. For those involved, the PDS concept is "becoming a way of thinking about teaching and learning and a way of involving everyone in the process" (Mantle-Bromley, 1998, p. 51). Mantle-Bromley asserts that this commitment centers around four core values:

◆ *Permanency.* The relationship is ongoing and persists even if key role players move on. The school site designates workspace and classroom space for formal instruction of novices. The university provides staff development as needed or requested by school personnel in order to accomplish PDS goals and objectives.

◆ *High Expectations.* All participants are held accountable for constant improvement individually and collectively. Novices are viewed as professionals and treated accordingly; the teacher mentors strive to identify and model best practice and to develop their coaching and mentoring skills.

◆ *Community.* All stakeholders strive to build trust and support as a community of learners. Trends in teacher education "envision the professional teacher as one who learns from teaching rather than as one who has finished learning how to teach" (Darling-Hammond, 1998, p. 7). Teacher mentors provide a needed support network to novices by reducing isolation and assisting with the planning and organizing of professional tasks.

◆ *Process of Renewal.* Participants in PDS see their school as a place for seeking better ways to improve personally and professionally. College instructors search for ways to make field experiences developmental and meaningful.

Cooperating teachers and peer mentors search for ways to guide novices without overwhelming them, administrators search for ways to expand teacher leadership and ownership, and beginners search for ways to connect with students, with peers, with teacher colleagues, and ultimately with their profession in a safe and supportive learning community.

WHAT DOES A COOPERATING TEACHER OR FIRST-YEAR PEER MENTOR DO?

As schools of education begin to revamp their programs, one thing is clear: there is a definite trend to place education majors in the field during most education courses. Why is this happening? First, teacher-education reform movements are focusing on the need for interns to have experiences in schools with diverse populations. Interns need to see teachers teaching in a way that "connects with students" and this requires "an understanding of differences that may arise from culture, family experiences, developed intelligences, and approaches to learning" (Darling-Hammond, 1998, p. 7). Secondly, interns need to experience different school levels (elementary, middle, and high) depending on their targeted certification level. These experiences provide firsthand knowledge about student characteristics, learners with exceptional needs, and students with various behavior problems. More important, interns have the opportunity to observe an experienced professional manage students in these settings. Finally, interns need to see different teaching styles and instructional strategies. They need to observe and dialogue about what it means to use different teaching strategies to accomplish various goals and objectives and how to assess and evaluate student achievement in their content area. Consequently, field-based experiences might be categorized in this way:

- *Short-Lab Visits.* As a result of teacher-education programs revamping their curriculums to include these initiatives, most upper-level undergraduate courses have a lab/field component. These school-site visits are targeted to certain schools and classrooms for specific reasons. Generally, these visits are scheduled for certain days and times over a quarter or semester.

- *Extended Field Experiences.* The first extended field visit a cooperating teacher may be asked to do is often called a "block" or "preinternship" visit. This visit generally averages four to six weeks, depending upon the length of the course. The intern is placed with a cooperating teacher for three to four hours a day during the experience. The cooperating teacher is asked to allow the intern to teach a unit to at least one class for 7 to 10 days. This field experience usually comes just before the quarter or semester that the intern is scheduled to do student teaching.

Student teaching, also called internship or apprenticeship, is the final performance assessment in most teacher-education programs. The intern is placed with a cooperating teacher for an entire quarter or semester, and the cooperating teacher is required to allow the intern to gradually assume all teaching responsibilities for at least three to five weeks.

♦ *First-Year Teaching.* Darling-Hammond (1998) reports that "more than 300 schools of education in the United States have created programs that extend beyond the traditional four-year bachelor's degree program, providing both education and subject-matter coursework that is integrated with clinical training in schools" (p. 8). Generally, this fifth year is a full-year school-based internship linked to graduate study on teaching and learning. Similarly, many school systems, recognizing the need to support first-year teachers, are assigning master teachers as mentors during the induction phase of new teachers' entry into teaching. If the school system is committed to this practice and has the resources, mentors might receive released time, specialized training, extra compensation, and/or stipends to assume these duties.

For example, in The TEACH Program designed by the Jefferson County School System in Birmingham, Alabama, master teachers are identified by building- or district-level administrators and are invited to leave their classrooms for a year to mentor three first-year teachers. One of the three first-year teachers is assigned to the mentor's classroom and the other two are placed in other vacancies in the school district. During the year, the peer mentor (a) models and team-teaches specific lessons, (b) teaches students while the first-year teacher observes in other classrooms or attends coaching sessions, and (c) makes regular and systematic classroom observations in order to help the first-year teacher reflect on practice and cope with professional duties and assignments.

To do this type of mentoring, first-year teachers work at half-salary; most do not see this as a detriment but rather as a paid extension of their teacher-preparation experience, as the program also includes advanced study at the graduate level. Mentors attend a two-day training session and can serve for a maximum of two years. They are required to meet regularly to share ideas and discuss concerns regarding their mentees.

Each of these experiences requires a different support role from cooperating teachers and peer mentors, and in some cases different types of knowledge and skills. We offer the following outline as a way to acquaint you with these roles so you can better target which support role appeals to you now and which one you can prepare for as you develop your coaching and mentoring skills.

Field Experience	Your Role	Knowledge and Skills
Short Labs		In a systematic effort to connect classroom learning with on-the-job experiences, teacher-education programs are requiring interns to take three- to five-hour labs in assigned schools in conjunction with specific education courses. The purpose is to introduce students to the various teaching roles and competencies targeted in the teacher preparation program.
	Classroom Expert	Your role is to do what you do best—TEACH. Students need to see best practice from competent facilitators of student learning. This doesn't mean that you are perfect, but it does imply that you are able to demonstrate effective teaching behaviors and classroom management procedures in areas such as: • Instructional planning • Presentation of subject matter and skills • Adjusting learning for individual differences • Communication skills • Managing student behavior • Diagnosing and assessing student achievement
	Level of Supervision	Students directed to your class for lab visitations generally will have a specific field observation assignment. The data they collect will be shared and discussed back in the college classroom. Your level of supervision will probably be limited to the time they spend in your classroom and whatever activities you decide to involve them in. You may be asked to complete a brief assessment of the students' interactions with you and your class.
Extended Field Visits		The extended four- to six-week field experience prior to student teaching provides interns with a good opportunity to get their feet wet before jumping into the ocean. Usually, this experience lasts half a day for a set period of time. During this phase, students get the opportunity to actually practice their ability to plan, teach, and manage a class for at least one full week.
	Classroom Expert	Your role is to demonstrate and discuss how you perform these tasks, offer opportunities for the intern to model you, and provide helpful suggestions in developing a successful performance.

Field Experience	*Your Role*	*Knowledge and Skills*
	Performance Coach	As a performance coach, you need to focus your feedback on targeted teaching behaviors, be descriptive and less judgmental when giving feedback, and help the intern become more competent by building from simple to more complex responsibilities.
	Level of Supervision	You will be asked to observe the intern during most teaching episodes and complete an assessment of performance that will be turned in to the college supervisor. The college supervisor will most often meet with you and the intern to discuss ratings and final grades. The college supervisor usually determines the course grade.
Student Teaching, Internship, or Apprenticeship		Most teacher-preparation programs are building a longer student teaching experience, lasting from 10 to 15 weeks. The intern must demonstrate the ability to plan, teach, and manage all of your classes for at least three to five weeks.
	Classroom Expert	Your role changes during each phase of the student-teaching experience depending on your assessment of the intern's abilities. The first few weeks of student teaching you will act as the classroom expert familiarizing the intern with your teaching style and classroom management system.
	Performance Coach	As a performance coach you need to be able to observe the intern, collect data, and dialog with the intern about selected teaching behaviors. Together you will collaboratively design the experience based on assessed needs.
	Student Support Teacher/ Mentor	As a mentor you need to be able to model professional growth and support the intern's professional development. This will require you to develop planned opportunities for monitoring the intern, providing descriptive feedback, checking for problems, and confronting and dealing with problems should they arise.

Field Experience	Your Role	Knowledge and Skills
	Level of Supervision	You will be asked to evaluate the overall performance of the intern for the entire student-teaching experience. The teacher preparation program will provide you with the summative evaluation instrument. Your assessment will be linked to the assessment made by the college supervisor. See Appendix A (page 173) for sample intern evaluation form.
First-Year Teacher Internship		In an ideal world, the first-year teacher is never left alone to sink or swim. Many school systems have developed beginning teacher mentor programs, which assign a peer mentor to help with career transition.
	Professional Role Model and Mentor	As a professional mentor, you are the vigilant lifeguard, watching for danger signs and ready to respond to calls for help. The goal is to provide moral support. However, as a mentor you need to be able to demonstrate all the roles just described based on the confidence level and proficiency of your mentee.
	Level of Supervision	In keeping with the intent of the program, peer mentors work collaboratively with mentees in a truly supportive role. Evaluation and supervision of the beginning teacher is usually left to the school administration.

SUMMARY

*"The most valuable gift you can give to
a colleague is a good example."*

—V. Estrem, 1993

You have been selected or assigned to be a cooperating teacher or a first-year peer mentor for several reasons. Chances are you are a professional who exhibits exceptional skills in these areas:

♦ Subject matter instruction

♦ Oral and written communication

♦ Interpersonal relationships

♦ Classroom management

♦ Multicultural sensitivity

♦ Flexibility

♦ Willingness to assume a redefined professional role

Your ability to function favorably in each of these areas will increase your success as a cooperating teacher or a peer mentor. We encourage you to seek information, sign up for staff development, or enroll in advanced higher education courses to increase both knowledge and skill in any area you identify as a growth target. Gordon (1991) points out that "the single greatest problem in mentoring programs that aren't functioning well is the lack of mentor preparation" (p. 31).

REFERENCES

Darling-Hammond, L. (1998). Teacher learning that supports student learning. *Educational Leadership*, 55(5), 6–11.

Gordon, S. (1991). *How to help beginning teachers succeed*. Alexandria, VA: Association for Supervision and Curriculum Development.

Mantle-Bromley, C. (1998). "A day in the life" at a professional development school. *Educational Leadership*, 55(5), 48–51.

Scherer, M. (1998). Perspectives: The importance of being a colleague. *Educational Leadership*, 55(5), 5.

COACHING BOOSTERS

Carver, C., & D.S. Katz. (2004). Teaching at the boundary of acceptable practice: What is a new teacher mentor to do? *Journal of Teacher Education*, 55(5), 449–462.

Kelley, L.M. (2004). Why induction matters. *Journal of Teacher Education*, 55(5), 438–448.

COMPETENCY TRAINING MODULES

COMPETENCY 1

UNDERSTANDING THE COACHING AND MENTORING ROLE

COMPETENCY STATEMENT

Acquire the knowledge and skills of an effective teacher mentor in order to provide systematic growth opportunities and support for student interns and beginning teachers over an extended period of time.

KNOWLEDGE BASE HIGHLIGHTS

- *Jonson, 2002:* "In the field of teaching, the mentor plays a vital and unique role in the development and training of someone new in the profession....The primary task, then, is to establish a relationship...based on mutual trust, respect, and collegiality."

- *Lipton & Wellman, 2003:* "Relationships matter. Who the mentor is and how she interacts with novices convey as strong a message as the content of the interactions. Skillful mentors provide appropriate supports to foster the novice's confidence for risk-taking."

- *Palmer, 1998:* "If we want to grow in our practice, we have two primary places to go: to the inner ground from which good teaching comes and to the community of fellow teachers from whom we can learn more about ourselves and our craft."

- *Rowley, 1999:* "As formal mentoring programs gain popularity, the need for identifying and preparing good mentors grows."

The term *mentor* had its origin in Homer's *Odyssey* when a wise and learned man named Mentor was entrusted with the education of Odysseus's son Telemachus. A central quality of mentoring is that it is intentional, nurturing, insightful, and supportive. The dictionary provides us with other terms for mentoring: guide, supporter, advisor, teacher specialist, teacher coach, consultant, helping teacher, peer teacher, support teacher, encourager, and befriender. Here's how several new teachers described their experiences with a mentorship program in their school district:

> When I found out I had a mentor, I thought my mentor would really be turned off by all my questions. Not only has my mentor always successfully answered my questions, but has continuously made me feel as though every question was pertinent to being a good teacher, even when I knew they weren't.

> The mentor program has helped me through some trying times. When I felt unsuccessful or that the students hated me, that I wasn't a help to them in any way, or even that I would never be a good teacher, my mentor always had some appropriate student/teacher story with which to cheer me. I feel that I am making progress toward being a "real teacher."

> My mentor helped me with so many management techniques—that's what new teachers need help with most of all! How do we manage all of this?

> For a new teacher, the biggest problem is managing all the information, getting to know the system, the building, the people, and the curriculum. No one can remember all that we are told in the orientation week at the beginning of the year. It takes time to get acclimated. New teachers simply must be patient with the information overload. It all becomes clear over time. What I found was, as my mentor told me, "As you need it, you can learn it." (Hicks & Huizinga, 1994)

These remarks from first-year teachers set the stage for what teacher mentoring is all about. As you read each example, you probably could feel the uncertainty and anxiousness of each new teacher. As a mentor, your role is to provide support and guidance in order to minimize these very common feelings. In today's volatile and competitive world, there are more demands being placed on teachers to help students achieve. This in turn is creating an environment where more and more educators, particularly those in school systems and teacher preparation programs, are beginning to look for guidance and direction in how to help student interns and beginning teachers perform to their best and choose to remain in the profession. (Boreen and Niday, 2003; Lucas, 1999; Brennan, Thames, & Roberts, 1999). Mentoring is viewed as a useful and bolstering tool for meeting challenges in today's workplace. In its most basic form, mentoring is way to help a less-experienced person find and develop their talents or skills. The literature on mentoring indicates that there are three basic types of mentoring:

◆ *Educational or academic mentoring* helps protégés improve their overall academic achievement. Many schools have established such programs to help at-risk students perform better in classrooms.

◆ *Career mentoring* helps proteges develop the necessary skills to enter or continue on a career path.

◆ *Personal development mentoring* supports protégés during times of personal or social stress and provides guidance for decision making.

Although we are primarily concerned with the second type of mentoring, career mentoring, our experiences show that you may encounter all three when working with student interns and beginning teachers.

PURPOSES FOR MENTORING

Sweeny (1994) tells us that "mentoring purposes vary from orientation, to induction, to instructional improvement, to an intent to change the culture of the school to a more collaborative learning environment." For our purposes, teacher mentoring focuses on three goals: (a) helping novices speed up the learning of a new job or skill and reduce the stress of transition; (b) improving instructional performance of novices through modeling by a top performer; and (c) socializing novices into the profession of teaching. You must decide, depending on the age, experience, and skills of the student intern or beginner teacher, which purpose has precedence.

MENTOR'S ROLES AND TASKS

The most difficult part of the process for both cooperating teachers and peer mentors is knowing what the mentoring role means. Sweeny (1994) points out that "the role must be well defined, especially if you have expectations for results." We suggest reviewing the terms listed at the beginning of this competency module and selecting the words that best fit you and the intent of the teacher-education or teacher-mentoring program. If you think of yourself as *a teacher coach* or a *support teacher,* you begin to define the role in terms of function. Once the role becomes clear, then the mentoring tasks also become more evident. As a *teacher coach* you might be involved in activities of observing performance, questioning the rationale for selected teaching behaviors, providing feedback for self-correction if needed, and modeling best practice. As a *support teacher* you might be involved as a buddy targeted to be available should questions or concerns arise.

As a mentor, you can't do it all. Part of your role necessitates helping mentees assess performance areas that are most critical for them. You need a sound understanding of the current frameworks for effective teaching (discussed in the Competency 2 module) in order to help novices diagnose both strengths and growth targets and a discerning eye to judge when they are ready to learn more complex teaching behaviors

(Jonson, 2002). The relationship between mentors and mentees needs to be collaborative. To facilitate this relationship, you must know your own strengths and weaknesses and be open to learning and working in partnership with college personnel and school colleagues.

SELECTION OF MENTORS

How are cooperating teacher and peer mentors selected? Most teacher-preparation staffs work with building-level administrators in outlining the qualities they seek in a cooperating teacher or first-year mentor teacher. The final choice usually rests with the building principal. As collaborative partnerships develop through professional development schools, the selection of mentors is evolving from "who's ready, willing, and able" to "what experienced teacher is the best match for a particular intern or entry-level teacher."

The literature base on mentoring purports that there are two approaches in selecting mentors: exclusive or inclusive. Exclusive approaches limit the choice to the best models of excellent instruction, rejecting other experienced teachers as "not good enough." The risks of these approaches include developing an "elite group" and perhaps an overemphasis on the technical skills of teachers. Using this mentoring approach may cause behaviors that are more divisive as teachers vie for status. It also tends to increase stress levels for all concerned when mentor teachers see the success of interns as reflecting on their teaching status.

Inclusive approaches seek to select as best models those teachers who are continual, life-long learners. This approach offers all veteran teachers the opportunity to be mentors, giving them the option to self-select out if and when the mentoring role becomes uncomfortable. Analogous to the thinking that sometimes the best teachers don't always become the best administrators, we know that some effective teachers do not always have the characteristics to be effective mentors. The mentor's role in this approach is to model professional growth, focus on improving the novice's teaching, and support the novice during the process. People skills and development of critical thinking are highly valued as a problem-solving process is fostered.

MENTOR QUALIFICATIONS

What does it take to be a good mentor? Gordon (1991) summarized the research based on effective mentors and concluded that the "most important characteristic of a successful mentor is a commitment to provide personal time and attention to the beginner" (p. 30). Nothing can be more demoralizing than a cooperating teacher or peer mentor scurrying around implying through body language and actions that he or she is too busy to set aside the time needed to focus on the novice.

Boreen and Niday (2003) surmised the qualities of strong mentors as: "(1) having mastered the basic skills of teaching; (2) understanding the need for flexibility in attitude and in practice; (3) recognizing that other teaching styles other than their own have merit; (4) realizing that possessiveness of student and classroom procedures is detrimental in the mentoring relationship; (5) being able to confront difficult situations with students, parents and colleagues skillfully; and (6) being able to articulate a professional vision beyond their own classroom" (p.10). Take a moment now and size up your qualifications.

COMPETENCY 1.1: MENTOR QUALIFICATIONS CHECKLIST

Rate yourself on each of the following characteristics as follows:

Effective Characteristics of Successful Mentors	High 3	Moderate 2	Low 1
Professional Demeanor			
1. Willingness to set aside time for mentee development			
2. Willing to be trained in mentoring			
3. Wide range of interests			
4. Positive view of people and teaching profession			
5. Confident in professional and personal realms			
6. Dependable and trustworthy			
7. Believes mentoring improves practice			
8. Feels comfortable observing peers			
9. Enjoys challenges and solving problems			
Highest Total = 27			
Competence and Experience			
1. Track record of high professional achievement			
2. Ability to work with adults as well as students			
3. Open to new ideas			
4. Adaptable in new situations			
5. Able to maneuver within and show influence in the system.			
6. Viewed by peers as professional and competent			
7. Highly skilled as a teacher in instructional skills and classroom management			
Highest Total = 21			

Communication Skills			
1. Good listener			
2. Demonstrates reflective questioning skills and approaches			
3. Can make a clear presentation of ideas			
4. Provides feedback in nonjudgmental ways			
5. Maintains confidentiality within the mentoring role			
Highest Total = 15			
Interpersonal Skills			
1. Congenial, accessible, and user friendly			
2. Genuine and sincere in helping others			
3. Inspires enthusiasm , hope and optimism			
4. Patient, helpful, and caring			
5. Collaborates well with colleagues			
6. Develops positive working relationship with novices			
Highest Total = 18			

Source: Podsen, I.J. (2002). *Teacher retention: What is your weakest link?* Larchmont, NY: Eye on Education , p. 114.

How did you do? Your selection as a mentor may be made by nomination from your peers or principal or you may choose to volunteer. Somewhere along the line the final choice will center on many of the characteristics listed above. Gordon (1991) concluded that "becoming a mentor should be represented as a prestigious role awarded to those whose possess outstanding credentials" (p. 29). We certainly agree. Do you?

MATCHING MENTEES AND MENTORS

STUDENT INTERNS

When matching student interns and cooperating teacher mentors, most field placement coordinators consider important the need to fill in any content or experience gaps in the intern's teacher-preparation program. Most extended field visitations before the full student-teaching internship attempt to provide teaching experience and exposure to particular grade levels, student populations, or content area specializations. Once this aspect has been reviewed, the coordinator for student field placements seeks schools and teachers to meet the profiles recommended by the college instructors for particular field placements. If a partnership with a particular school is not in place, the final selection is left to the principal who does the recruiting of cooperating teachers and matching with interns. Usually, the matching criteria are grade level and content area (Jonson, 2002).

When partnerships are in place, college instructors work closely with schools, getting to know the teaching staff and principals, and collaborating with them about designing intern experiences. The college instructors, armed with data about specific groups of interns, now meet with principals, and together they match interns and mentors in order to create the best partnership. Matching in these situations also takes into account teaching styles and the degree of nurturing needed by an intern, in addition to grade level and content factors. Mentors and mentees usually make the final decision to remain together or seek another partner if the initial match proves to be unproductive.

ENTRY-LEVEL TEACHERS

In matching peer mentors with beginning teachers, Huffman and Leak (1986) indicate that beginning teachers favored mentors who teach similar grade levels or content matter. But the strongest desire expressed was having a competent mentor rather than one less competent, no matter what the grade level or subject matter. Gordon (1991) asserts that best matches take into consideration personality and educational philosophy compatibility. This tells us that informal opportunities for mentors and mentees to get to know one another need to be considered so their matching preferences can be used in the decision-making process. See Appendix B page 178 for an example of a Mentor/Mentee Matching Preference Inventory.

TRAINING AND SUPPORT FOR MENTORING

The best mentoring programs provide specific training for all mentors (Jonson, 2002). Ideally, Sweeny (1994) suggests that a school district should train all teachers interested in serving as cooperating teachers and peer mentors, thereby building an inclusive pool of trained enthusiasts. As we pointed out earlier, good teachers of children do not necessarily make good mentors of adults. There are many skills needed to work with adults that are not learned in the classroom. However, for many school systems, this training may not be financially possible.

So what are the choices? The first place to look is within your local college, university, or state department of education. In Georgia, for example, teachers interested in working with student interns are encouraged to seek endorsement as a Teacher Support Specialist (TSS). This endorsement provides the necessary training and skills to mentor an intern, and the state offers a stipend each time a trained teacher agrees to work with a student teacher. Another place to check is the Mentoring Leadership and Resource Network on the Internet. This network receives a modest grant from the Association of Supervision and Curriculum Development (ASCD) to promote the mentoring and induction of new teachers by supporting mentors and mentoring programs in K-12 schools. This resource offers practical tips, suggestions, and information about this critical topic (http://www.mentors.net/Library.html).

Schools accepting student interns might consider creating support groups among those teachers selected to be cooperating teachers or peer mentors. Working with the school administration, these support groups of teacher mentors become part of a systematic induction team to guide both student interns and first-year teachers into the profession. The purpose of these groups is to discover, discuss, refine, and formalize their growing knowledge about mentoring practices. Principals could then use this information to design staff development opportunities for both novices and mentors.

BENEFITS FOR ALL

THE STUDENT INTERN

Early exposure to competent teachers in the field through field labs and extended classroom experiences provide interns with concrete examples to link theory learned in college to current situations in today's classrooms. Interns learn more by seeing effective practice modeled and getting incremental opportunities to try out teaching behaviors required in their specific content area or level of specialization. Such exposure assists in preparing for job transfer as each experience builds on the previous one, requiring the intern to reflect and assess progress based on specific criteria, performance standards, and feedback from K-12 professionals.

THE COOPERATING TEACHER MENTOR

The teaching profession is not particularly known for offering rewards for effective teachers. Most pay scales show the highest raises occur in the first half of one's teaching career, and there are few opportunities to recognize the efforts and impact of master teachers. Any job has the potential of stagnation and burnout unless infused with new energy and meaningful purpose. One way to offset stagnation is to offer seasoned veterans the opportunity to renew themselves professionally by nurturing and supporting novices.

ENTRY-LEVEL TEACHERS

Effective teacher mentoring can eliminate or significantly reduce the number of problems faced by beginning teachers. School systems and university teacher-education programs involved in team approaches to teacher induction find that novices show significantly better performance and more positive attitudes and perceptions about teaching than those not involved in some type of structured mentoring program (Henry, 1988). Gordon (1991) reports that beginning teachers indicated that their peer mentors provided help in such areas as location of instructional materials, classroom management, lesson planning, assessing and grading students, establishing realistic expectations of student work and behavior, and having someone to talk to who would listen to their concerns. This assistance addresses many of the risk factors that often lead first-year teachers to leave the profession.

PEER MENTORS

In a fully developed teacher-mentoring program, master teachers get the opportunity to emerge from their isolated classrooms and see what's going on in their schools and even in their school district. The specialized mentor training provides an infusion of new knowledge and skills, which often revitalizes one's personal and professional growth. One former mentor commented, "After serving as a peer mentor last year, I returned to my classroom with a refreshed and renewed attitude. Being away from the classroom and working with first-year teachers helped me to reflect on what I did as a teacher and why. This reflection led to better ideas and the creation of a more positive learning situation for my students this year." Overall, both cooperating teachers and peer mentors report that the process is beneficial to them, saying it helped them to grow professionally, develop a clearer idea of effective teaching, and understand the importance of effective interaction and collaboration skills (Hawk, 1987; Odell, 1990).

CONTEXT FOR MENTORING IN SCHOOLS

Learning to be a good mentor and doing mentoring takes time. Be patient with yourself and the process. Finding the time in your already busy schedule will always be a factor. Having a supportive principal is generally the key to how successful any program will be at the school level.

As a mentor, you need ongoing organizational and technical backing. A regular schedule of seminars for mentors is suggested as a way to provide mutual support and assistance, so mentors can share problems and successful strategies for mentoring novices. Mentors also require released time to plan support activities, observe novices and provide feedback, gather instructional resources, and team-teach lessons to demonstrate effective teaching approaches. For first-year peer mentors in particular, "the addition of these responsibilities onto an already hectic work schedule is a disservice to the mentor and will significantly impact the quality of support to the first-year teacher" (Gordon, 1991, p. 38). Here are some things to discuss with your principal:

♦ Substitute time in order to mentor your mentee. Sweeny (1994) recommends one day per month used in half-day blocks.

♦ Incentives for mentors such as: release time from supervision duty, opportunity to attend a conference or workshop with the mentee, reduced number of teaching classes, tuition for graduate work targeted for mentor training, and some form of formal recognition through merit pay, certificates, and plaques.

♦ Formal recognition of the contributions made by both cooperating teacher and peer mentors.

Rowley (1999) reinforces this notion by asserting that "although the majority of mentor teachers would do this important work without compensation, we must not overlook the relationship between compensation and commitment. Programs that provide mentors with a stipend, release time from extra duties, or additional opportunities for professional growth make important statements about the value of the work and its significance in the school community" (p. 20).

TEACHER-MENTORING PROGRAM EVALUATION

We know effective programs involve a cycle of planning, implementing, and assessing results and using such results to renew planning for improvement. We encourage mentors and cooperating teachers to seek feedback about their mentoring skills and school officials and college instructors to study the effects of teacher mentoring in their respective school districts or teacher-education programs. Such program evaluation could yield valuable data and suggest alternative approaches to improve teacher-mentoring programs. Here are two evaluation tools that may be useful.

COMPETENCY 1.2:
MENTOR TEACHER EVALUATION

Dear Mentee:

Like you, I am learning more about being an effective teacher. Part of my professional responsibility is assisting you to develop your teaching and classroom management skills. To help me learn how I can do this better, I need feedback from you about how I am performing as your mentor teacher. Please mark the column that best describes your viewpoint.

1. You need more knowledge and/or skill in this area.
2. You might need more knowledge and/or skill in this area. I am experiencing problems and/or some things are still not clear.
3. You are doing well in this area. I'm not having any consistent problems.
4. You are doing a very good job. I understand everything clearly.
5. You are doing an outstanding job. I have learned a lot, and you have helped me to transfer these skills into my teaching.

Skill Descriptors	*1*	*2*	*3*	*4*	*5*
1. Ability to develop a positive, nurturing working relationship as a mentor. (C1, C2)					
2. Ability to be open to new ideas, methods, techniques, and professional responsibilities. (C1, C2, C8)					
3. Ability to sequence your teaching tasks based on your needs, strengths, and concerns. (C2)					
4. Ability to assist you in developing a plan to increase your teaching and classroom management skills. (C2)					
5. Ability to provide support and guidance as you practice and learn new information and skills. (C3)					
6. Ability to help you diagnose your strengths and growth areas accurately. (C3)					
7. Ability to provide timely, descriptive, and specific feedback on your performance to help you self-correct. (C4)					

Skill Descriptors	1	2	3	4	5
8. Ability to help you analyze your performance and identify alternatives in a conference setting. (C4)					
9. Ability to demonstrate effective teaching practices in the classroom. (C5)					
10. Ability to demonstrate effective classroom management practices. (C6)					
11. Ability to show teaching strategies that address cultural diversity, language differences, and various learning styles among students. (C7)					
12. Ability to demonstrate high ethical perspectives and professional contributions to the school, the district, and the profession. (C8)					
13. Ability to set and meet regular meeting times to discuss your concerns. (C2)					

Comments:

We have indicated in parentheses which training modules address the skill descriptors should you want additional information or resources. We also encourage the mentor to self-assess and then compare the ratings with those of the mentee as a way to identify strengths and growth areas as they relate to the qualities of a good mentor.

COMPETENCY 1.3:
TEACHER-MENTORING
PROGRAM EVALUATION

Here are some questions to guide the assessment of teacher-mentoring programs in schools. They should stimulate discussion, suggest data-collection methods, and identify individuals responsible for gathering the information.

Assessment Criteria	*Discussion Outcomes*
1. What effect has the teacher-mentor program had on the following areas and/or individuals? • Instructional improvement • Professional relationships within the school • School-community relations • Administrative support for staff development • Student interns • First-year teachers • Cooperating teacher and peer mentors • Teacher preparation program	
2. Have the needs of student interns, first-year teachers, and mentors been assessed? What are they and how have they been addressed?	
3. Have adequate organizational, technical, and effective support resources been provided for cooperating teacher and/or peer mentors? What has been provided?	
4. Have student interns, beginning teachers, mentors, and school staff been sufficiently prepared for their roles in the teacher-mentoring program?	
5. Have clear goals and objectives for novices and mentors been identified and achieved? How will the quality of the mentoring experience be assessed?	
6. What positive or negative unintended outcomes have emerged as a result of this novice assistance program for student interns and/or first-year teachers?	

SUMMARY

"To furnish the means of acquiring knowledge is...
the greatest benefit that can be conferred upon mankind."

John Quincy Adams
(V. Caruana, 1998)

Coaching and mentoring a colleague can be a beneficial experience for both mentors and mentees. The key to mentoring is a strong one-to-one relationship between the partners. Within the context of career mentoring, the process provides novices a link to the working world of teachers and school communities. Sweeny (1992) gives us these tips for beginning mentors:

♦ Be positive and supportive. Save the war stories.

♦ Timing of advice is critical. Wait until novices express the need.

♦ Be willing to back off. Don't get defensive if novices don't accept an idea or an approach. Just because it works for you may not mean it will work for them.

♦ Keep the relationship confidential. Your peers don't need to know every success or failure.

♦ Plan ahead so you can be available when approached for help.

♦ Listen to the novices' concerns. They may seem unimportant to you, but they are important to the novices.

♦ Encourage novices to reflect and question their performance. Take the time to debrief every teaching episode, challenging mentees to explain how and why they performed a particular behavior.

♦ Plan ways to get to know mentees outside the school. This allows for more sharing and building of trust. It communicates to them that they are important and you like them as individuals.

Material in this chapter was adapted from Sweeny, B. (1994, Spring). *A new teacher mentoring knowledge base of best practices: A summary of lessons learned from practitioners.* MLRN Mentoring Library, vol. 3 no. 2.

REFERENCES

Boreen, J., & D. Niday. (2003). *Mentoring across boundaries: Helping beginning teachers succeed in challenging situations.* Portland, MA: Stenhouse Publishers.

Brennan, S., W. Thames, & R. Roberts. (1999). Mentoring with a mission. *Educational Leadership*, 56(8), 49–52.

Gordon, S. (1991). *How to help beginning teachers succeed.* Alexandria, VA: Association for Supervision and Curriculum Development.

Hawk, P. (1987). Beginning teacher programs: Benefits for the experienced educator. *Action in Teacher Education*, 8(4), 59–63.

Henry, M. A. (1988). *Project credit: Certification renewal experiences designed to improve teaching.* Terre Haute, IN: Indiana State University, Department of Secondary Education. ERIC Document Reproduction Service No. ED 291 681.

Hicks, A., & J. Huizinga. (1994, Fall). *Protégé reflections: What new teachers say.* MLRN Mentoring Library, vol. 3 no. 3.

Huffman, G., & S. Leak. (1986). Beginning teachers' perceptions of mentors. *Journal of Teacher Education*, 37(1), 22–24.

Jonson, K. (2002). *Being an effective mentor: How to help beginning teachers succeed.* Thousand Oaks, CA: Corwin Press, Inc.

Lipton, L., & B. Wellman. (2003). *Making mentoring work.* Alexandria, VA: Association for Supervision and Curriculum Development.

Lucas, A. (1999). Developing competent practitioners. *Educational Leadership*, 56(8), 45–48.

Odell, S. J. (1990). A collaborative approach to teacher induction that works. *The Journal of Staff Development*, 11(4), 12–16.

Palmer, P. J. (1998). *The courage to teach.* San Francisco: Jossey-Bass.

Rowley, J. (1999). The good mentor. *Educational Leadership*, 56(8), 20–22.

Stedman, P., & S. A. Stoot (1998). Teachers helping teachers. *Educational Leadership*, 55(5), 37–39.

Sweeny, B. (1992, Winter). *Advice to beginning mentors.* MLRN Mentoring Library, vol. 1 no. 1.

Sweeny, B. (1994, Spring). *A new teacher mentoring knowledge base of best practices: a summary of lessons learned from practitioners.* MLRN Mentoring Library, vol. 3 no. 2.

COACHING BOOSTERS

Hargreaves, A., & M. Fullan. (2000, Winter). Mentoring in the new millennium. *Theory Into Practice,*39(1), 50–56.

Niday, D., & J. Boreen. (2003) *Mentoring: Guiding, coaching, and sustaining beginning teachers.* Videocassettes. Portland, MA: Stenhouse Publishers.

Sweeny, B. (1999). Mentoring to improve schools. Videocassettes. Alexandria, VA: Association for Supervision and Curriculum Development.

COMPETENCY 2

PROMOTING COLLABORATIVE LEARNING

COMPETENCY STATEMENT

Model, develop, and maintain a coactive and collegial relationship with teacher interns, beginning teachers, peers and supervisors.

KNOWLEDGE BASE HIGHLIGHTS

- *Darling-Hammond, 1998:* "Teachers learn best by studying, doing, and reflecting; by collaborating with other teachers; by looking closely at students and their work; and by sharing what they see."

- *Johnson & Kardos, 2005:* "To make substantive improvement in teaching and learning, a school must draw on the professional knowledge and skills that experienced teachers have accumulated and refined over the years." Principals must bring veteran and beginning teachers together as a learning community.

- *Jonson, 2002:* Mentors need to be able to communicate openly with beginning teachers. "Being open means being willing to share experiences and materials without reserve....It is crucial that the mentor model for the new teacher the importance of continuing education by partaking in further learning."

- *Portner, 2002:* "Mentoring takes place within a working relationship, and the development of a working relationship requires active participation of both its parties."

CREATING A CONNECTION

In his book, *How to Help Beginning Teachers Succeed*, Stephen Gordon tells us to "celebrate the beginner's arrival." Your principal can really help you with this aspect by setting up a coffee or a luncheon to help interns and first-year teachers meet the entire staff or team. One administrator announced the arrival of student interns from the local college to the entire school community by placing a welcome greeting on the outside message board. An information packet about the school, including a student handbook, a list of faculty with room numbers, a map of the school, and other general information, helps novices to feel a part of the professional community. Then, you, the cooperating teacher or peer mentor, could follow this up with a brief orientation to the school in order to answer any questions and to assess your mentee's anxiety level.

GETTING TO KNOW YOUR MENTEE

It's up to you to establish rapport and start building trust. A good way to start is by setting aside time for a short private interview to get to know the individual. This first conversation will set the stage for what is to come. Select an informal location that is free of interruptions. To create an open and comfortable dialog, consider these tips:

- ♦ Greet your mentee warmly with a handshake and a smile.

- ♦ Make small talk and use humor.

- ♦ Learn about your mentee by asking questions about his or her interests, backgrounds, and experiences.

Here's a proposed guideline for your first meeting. Use these questions as a way to get to know your mentee.

COMPETENCY 2.1:
COOPERATING TEACHER-MENTOR
INTERVIEW GUIDE

Beginning the Conversation

(Get a feel for your intern's experiences and insights. Let him or her talk about personal background and career aspirations. Get an overview of his/her teacher-preparation program. Jot down notes to help you remember specific points that you feel are important.)

Here are some questions that you might ask:

♦ What field experiences have you had with teachers and students? What did you learn?

♦ Why do you want to be a teacher? What subjects do you plan to teach? Tell me about your teacher-preparation program. What other courses or job responsibilities do you have this quarter/semester?

Middle of Conversation (Begin to focus on task.)

♦ Have you become acquainted with the physical layout of the school? What are your first impressions of our school?

♦ What would you say are your teaching strengths? What teaching responsibilities are you concerned about? What ideas do you have to address these concerns?

♦ What is your understanding of what is expected of you during your field experience? What classroom experiences do you feel you need in order to develop your skills?

♦ What kind of support from me would you find helpful? How has your college supervisor helped you?

End of Conversation (Share information about yourself.)

♦ Tell your intern a little about yourself and why you agreed to be a cooperating teacher. Be positive and optimistic.

♦ Describe your students and summarize your own teaching strengths and areas you are working to improve.

♦ Set the stage for a team experience by collaboratively establishing a routine time for you both to share information, questions, and concerns. Tell the intern how you prefer to be contacted, especially at home, if this is an option.

COMPETENCY 2.2:
FIRST-YEAR PEER-MENTOR
INTERVIEW GUIDE

Beginning the Conversation

(Get a feel for your beginner's experiences and insights. Let him or her talk about personal background and career aspirations. Get an overview of his/her teacher-preparation program. Jot down notes to help you remember specific points that you feel are important.)

Here are some questions that you might ask:

♦ What experiences have you had with teachers and students? Describe your student-teaching experience. What did you learn?

♦ Why do you want to be a teacher? Tell me about your teacher-preparation program. What other responsibilities, professionally or personally, do you have?

Middle of Conversation (Begin to focus on task.)

♦ What would you say are your teaching strengths? What teaching responsibilities are you concerned about? What ideas do you have to address these concerns?

♦ Have you planned your first week of school? What can I do to help you during the first two weeks both with instructional needs and managing students?

♦ What kind of support from me would you find helpful? How often would you like to meet so we can discuss your concerns and plan ahead?

End of Conversation (Share information about yourself.)

♦ Tell your mentee a little about yourself and why you agreed to be a peer mentor. Be positive and optimistic.

♦ Describe your students and summarize your own teaching strengths and areas you are working to improve.

♦ Set the stage for a team experience by collaboratively establishing a routine time for you both to share information, questions, and concerns.

♦ Talk about the purpose and goals of the mentoring program.

PLANNING FOR SUCCESS—CLARITY OF PURPOSE

Failing to plan is planning to fail.

The next conversation with your mentee should center on discussing specific goals and objectives about the novice's performance. Here's where you identify the team mission—successful teaching of a unit of study for a specific length of time, under certain conditions. The important thing is to clarify who does what and when, who sets goals, and who establishes a set time for sharing and reflecting. A good way to think about this may be as follows: You, as the mentor teacher, need to be as clear about performance criteria and methods as you expect the novice to be about lesson plans and assessment of those plans (Boreen & Niday, 2003).

Now to help guide you in this area, you have several options. You can ask the mentee for past data about his or her performance and the criteria used to assess it during his/her coursework. It is likely that the novice has received feedback from course instructors about specific aspects of the teaching process. If you can live with the criteria used by the teacher-preparation program, then your comments will build on that conceptual framework. Another option is to use the teacher assessment instrument utilized at your school; this one should be very familiar to you. A third choice is tapping into the professional literature and finding what's current. For example, nationally prominent organizations have developed sets of standards primarily for student interns and first-year teachers. The Interstate New Teacher Assessment and Support Consortium (INTASC) has devised standards compatible with the National Board for Professional Teaching Standards (NBPTS), and the Association for Supervision and Curriculum Development (ASCD) has a framework for professional practice.

The bottom line is this: When novice teachers meet with experienced veterans, they both need a framework to determine which aspect of teaching requires their attention. "Without a framework, the structure is reduced to something the cooperating teacher or peer mentor has in his/her head, and thus reflects the personal beliefs that individual holds about teaching, regardless of whether these have ever been made explicit. With a framework of professional practice in hand, the participants can conduct conversations about where to focus improvement efforts within the context of shared definitions and values" (Danielson, 1996, p. 7). Exhibit 2.1 is a brief outline of ASCD's standards for competent teaching as developed by Charlotte Danielson.

What is important for you to know is that most colleges and universities are using these frameworks to design or restructure their teacher education programs. Follow-up on these standards can only increase consistent communication between you and your mentee and reduce an unsystematic approach to a very complex process. In addition, they offer specific descriptions to help you describe the performance in nonthreatening terms. The Association for Supervision and Curriculum Development's Web site has further details: http://www.ascd.org.

EXHIBIT 2.1. A FRAMEWORK FOR PROFESSIONAL PRACTICE

- Domain 1: Planning and Preparation

  Components:

  1a: Demonstrating knowledge of content and pedagogy

  1b: Demonstrating knowledge of students

  1c: Selecting instructional goals

  1d Demonstrating knowledge of resources

  1e: Designing coherent instruction

  1f: Assessing student learning

- Domain 2: Classroom Environment

  Components:

  2a: Creating an environment of respect

  2b: Establishing a culture for learning

  2c: Managing classroom procedures

  2d: Managing student behavior

  2e: Organizing physical space

- Domain 3: Instruction

  Components:

  3a: Communicating clearly and accurately

  3b: Using questioning and discussion techniques

  3c: Engaging students in learning

  3d: Providing feedback to students

  3e: Demonstrating flexibility

- Domain 4: Professional Responsibilities

  Components:

  4a: Reflecting on teaching

  4b: Maintaining records

  4c: Communicating with families

  4d: Contributing to the school and district

  4e: Growing and developing professionally

  4f: Showing professionalism

A review of the criteria agreed upon sets up a common dialog between you and your mentee. It helps you to reexamine what you do unconsciously, and it focuses you on the task. Use the framework as a way to stimulate conversation about the various aspects of teaching and to analyze current performance strengths and growth areas. Once you have a clear idea of the novice's self-assessment on these indicators, then collaborate on a plan to address them. Here's a suggested format.

COMPETENCY 2.3: PLANNING GUIDE

Mentee: _____

Mentor Teacher: _____

Week of: _____

Instructional Improvement Goal

Domain: _____ Component: _____

Objective(s):

_____

_____

_____

Action Plan

Mentee's Responsibilities:

_____

_____

Mentor's Responsibilities:

_____

_____

Standard of Achievement:

_____

_____

Reflection

Mentee's Assessment

_____

Mentor's Assessment:

_____

IMPROVING YOUR FACILITATION SKILLS

Be the guide on the side rather than the sage on the stage.

To really know how skillful you are in the area of collaborative relationships, you must find out how others see you. One of the hazards of being a coach is coming across as if your ideas are the only way to teach. The student intern, more than a beginning teacher, perceives this as: "I better do it this way, or else I won't get a good recommendation or course grade." Effective communication depends on your ability to minimize any barriers. Bolton (1986) suggests that such roadblocks to communication can be detrimental to building a team because they tend to "trigger defensiveness, resistance and resentment" (p. 15). Gordon (1970) identifies 12 barriers to successful interpersonal communication:

EXHIBIT 2.2. COMMUNICATION BARRIERS

Barrier	Description	Example
1. Criticizing	Making a negative evaluation of the novice.	"You've brought this on yourself—you've got no one else to blame."
2. Name calling	Putting down or stereotyping the novice.	"All beginners are just alike!"
3. Diagnosing	Analyzing why the novice is behaving as he or she is; playing amateur psychiatrist.	"Just because you have had courses on more current curriculum in college doesn't mean you know what is best."
4. Praising evaluatively	Making a positive judgement about the novice.	"You are a perfect role model."
5. Ordering	Commanding the person to do what you want to have done.	"I want those bulletin boards changed by tomorrow."
6. Threatening	Trying to control the novice's actions by warning of a negative consequence.	"Attend the PTO meeting tonight or I'll report this to your supervisor."
7. Moralizing	Tell the novice what he should do; preaching.	"You should cut your hair—it's too long."
8. Excessive questioning	Asking closed questions.	"Did you spend much time on your lesson plans?"

Barrier	Description	Example
9. Advising	Giving the novice a solution to his or her problem.	"If I were you, I'd tell the parents...."
10. Diverting	Pushing the novice's problems aside through distraction.	"You think you're tired? Let me tell you about when I was a...."
11. Logical argument	Attempting to convince the novice with an appeal to facts or logic without consideration of the emotional factors involved.	"Look at the facts. If you hadn't been absent yesterday, the unit would be completed."
12. Reassuring	Trying to stop the other person from feeling the negative emotions he or she is experiencing.	"Don't worry about that lesson. You will still pass the course."

The 12 barriers are viewed as high-risk responses; instead of promoting communication between you and the mentee, the 12 barriers can actually "block conversation, thwart the other person's problem-solving efficiency, and increase the emotional distance between people" (Bolton, 1986).

As the mentoring teacher it will be difficult not to praise evaluatively (4), offer advice (9), and reassure (12). After all, you ask, aren't you supposed to praise, guide, and reassure? The answer is yes, but not when the novice is stressed, overly anxious about teaching, or experiencing personal problems. Why? Because these responses to a mentee can "trigger feelings of inadequacy, anger or promote a dependency" toward you (Bolton, 1986). The novice could become rebellious and argumentative if you resort to such behaviors, especially criticizing, diagnosing, or ordering.

These 12 roadblocks to communication are very common and habitual ways of responding to anyone in a conversation. To communicate effectively with your mentee, you must be cognizant of the risks these barriers may have on your relationship and learn to avoid them.

To determine your communication style and minimize any communication roadblocks, you might respond first and then ask a trusted colleague to give you feedback on these questions.

COMPETENCY 2.4:
COMMUNICATION INVENTORY

Communication Behavior	Often	Sometimes	Rarely
1. Do I come across in a judgmental way in my day-to-day interactions with team members?			
2. Do I put down or ignore others in group discussions?			
3. Do I focus on the weak qualities of coworkers rather than on strong points?			
4. Do I interrupt often to interject my opinion?			
5. Do I fail to restate the ideas or suggestions of others to show that I have heard them?			
6. Do I come across too strongly when expressing my opinion or idea?			
7. Do I speak often preventing others from having equal opportunity to express their ideas?			
8. Do I criticize or try to change the opinion of others?			
9. Do I overlook involving the entire group's members in the discussion, actively seeking their input, especially if they are quiet?			
10. Do I use sarcasm in my daily interactions?			
11. Do I show impatience as I wait for another person to finish talking?			
12. Do I suggest a solution before the speaker fully describes the situation or problem?			
13. Do I nonverbally show disinterest in a speaker by looking bored, losing eye contact, shuffling papers, etc.?			
14. Do I misinterpret what was said because I'm mentally preparing my response?			

If you answered *often* to any of these questions, you may want to seek additional feedback about your listening skills and find ways to improve them. The goal of seeking feedback on your communication patterns is to make sure that you are able to develop a collaborative style that fosters openness and trust. An overbearing or domineering model may prevent your intern from developing his or her teaching style.

FOSTERING OPEN DIALOG

Novices, in general, have just scratched the surface in learning how to design an effective lesson, deliver it, and manage a class. Encourage student interns or first-year teachers to talk aloud about a specific teaching behavior such as how the lesson was planned or how they plan to teach the lesson. Use open-ended questions to challenge their ideas. To draw out novices' thoughts, use phrases beginning with what, how, describe, explain, justify, or illustrate. Try to get them to critically assess their methods and procedures before suggesting more effective or appropriate techniques. This doesn't mean that you let them proceed if their plan will set them up for a problem.

Remember, as a cooperating teacher mentor it's your classroom and you are ultimately responsible for what happens; as a peer mentor you are not ultimately responsible, but prevention is the key to success for first-year teachers. The trend in teacher preparation is to dialogue with beginners before a teaching episode, and then after the lesson is taught, in order to develop complex teaching behaviors through interactive coaching. To do this, you must have effective listening skills. Communication experts suggest maintaining good eye contact without staring and leaning forward toward the mentee to show interest and concern. Avoid interrupting, and paraphrase to clarify your understanding. Use your knowledge of nonverbal behavior to assess the feelings of your mentee as well as the message content. In intercultural situations, you may have to adapt your communication style to show respect for another's culture. If you're not sure, ASK!

RESERVING CRITICISM AND JUDGMENT

Creating a learning climate of acceptance is often easier said than done, especially if the mentee is tentative and lacks skills you expect them to have. The goal is to convey the notion that all problems can be handled and that a positive outcome can occur even when mistakes are made. Few beginners complete their field experiences without expressing that they could have done some things better. If we prejudge interns and first-year teachers, we may limit the opportunities we could provide, or, worse, they may plod through the experience living in fear of making a mistake and losing your support.

Begin by examining your own conventionalized ideas of things and people. You may believe that you have none, but let's make sure. Prejudgments are often views we hold based on cultural values, experiences, or stereotypes, and may include such opinions as:

- ◆ Cooperative learning is a waste of time.
- ◆ Lecturing is the best method to teach content.
- ◆ Women are better teachers than men.
- ◆ Special education students just don't belong in the regular classroom.
- ◆ Teaching an interdisciplinary unit isn't worth the time and effort.
- ◆ Minority students are usually discipline problems.

The point we are making is that as you mentor various interns and beginning teachers, you are going to confront the values and beliefs of a diverse group of young adults. The first step is for you to clarify your own values and beliefs and to see how these factors have shaped you as a teacher. It is important to see how these belief systems make you different and how they may not be seen as "right" or be easily understood by a mentee. By doing this, you will recognize the need for others to connect with and value their own beliefs. As a mentor, you can then help the beginners to do the same by actively welcoming their viewpoints, even if they vary from your own.

Effective mentors are able to recognize the strengths of novices by utilizing the talents, skills, and cultural knowledge they bring to the teaching situation. "Inexperienced" doesn't always mean less knowledgeable or less competent. Recognizing different teaching styles and exploring ways to use these styles in the classroom helps to build mutual support and respect, even if they're different than your teaching practices.

EXERCISE 2.1. THROUGH THE LOOKING GLASS

Let's take a moment to jot down your views on the following subjects. Try to identify any stereotypical lenses you may be using. Here are some categories to begin your analysis. Add some of your own to consider.

Categories	Value or Belief	Impact on My Teaching
1. Parent involvement		
2. Homework		
3. Peer tutoring		
4. Cooperative learning		
5. Interdisciplinary learning		
6. Mainstreaming		
7. Team teaching		
8. Lesson plans		

Categories	Value or Belief	Impact on My Teaching
9. Time-out rooms		
10. Inclusion classrooms		
11. Writing across the curriculum		
12. Multiculturalism		
13. Effective teaching		
14. Motivating students to learn		

DEALING WITH CONFLICT

Conflict is part of any dynamic organization, usually arising because individuals care and want to do their jobs well. As a coach and mentor, you want to show the way when it comes to effectively working through a problem because it helps to build stronger working relationships. Part of a mentor's job is to be a professional role model. One of the most important skills you can help a novice develop is his or her ability to deal with conflict—with peers, students, parents, and even with yourself. The process of conflict resolution needs to be discussed at the very beginning of the mentoring experience.

CONFLICT DEFINED

According to the Office of Dispute Resolution (2004), conflict happens when two people disagree about something. Despite the fact that people have a lot of similarities, since each of us is different from everybody else, we will have conflicts. Conflict is a natural part of life; it happens to us often.

Conflict can be positive and beneficial, as well as a learning and growing experience. When we deal with it in a constructive way, we can generally find a solution that satisfies all parties. This is what we call managing or dealing successfully with conflict. Unfortunately, conflict also has its negative side—A side that can sometimes result in disagreements, hurt feelings and broken relationships. The purpose of this discussion is to show you that there are options for finding a better way to manage and confront disagreements.

CONFLICT APPROACHES

There are three primary strategies that we use to deal with conflict:

1. **Flight**—Avoiding conflict and hoping that it will go away.
2. **Fight**—Using authority, rights or force to attempt to prevail over others.

3. **Unite**—Talking with other people to develop solutions that will satisfy mutual interests—some result that they all can "live with."

All of these approaches are acceptable depending on the situation. The skill is to know when and how to use these strategies at the appropriate time. Heathfield (2002) tells us that, "if you are like many people, you avoid conflict in your daily work life. You see only the negative results of conflict." However, effectively managed conflict has many payoffs for both you and your school organization.

The professional literature on conflict resolution outlines the following styles as the behaviors we most often demonstrate in dealing with conflict.

- *Competing* is assertive and uncooperative—an individual pursues his or her own concerns at the other person's expense. **Fight**

- *Accommodating* is unassertive and cooperative—the opposite of competing. When accommodating, an individual neglects his/her own concerns to satisfy the concerns of the other person; there is an element of self-sacrifice in this mode. **Flight**

- *Avoiding* is unassertive and uncooperative—the individual does not immediately pursue his or her own concerns or those of the other person. He or she does not address the conflict. Avoiding might take the form of diplomatically sidestepping an issue, postponing an issue until a better time, or simply withdrawing from a threatening situation. **Flight**

- *Collaborating* is both assertive and cooperative—the opposite of avoiding. Collaborating involves an attempt to work with the other person to find some solution that fully satisfies the concerns of both persons. It means digging into an issue to identify the underlying concerns of the two individuals and to find an alternative that meets both sets of concerns. **Unite**

- *Compromising* is intermediate in both assertiveness and cooperativeness. The objective is to find some expedient, mutually acceptable solution that partially satisfies both parties. It falls on a middle ground between competing and accommodating. Compromising gives up more than competing, but less than accommodating. Likewise, it addresses an issue more directly than avoiding, but doesn't explore it in as much depth as collaborating. Compromising might mean splitting the difference, exchanging, making concessions, or seeking a quick middle-ground position. **Unite**

(Excerpted and adapted from *Responses to Conflict:* http://p2001.health.org/CTW06/mod3tr.htm)

EXERCISE 2.2. ASSESSING YOUR CONFLICT MANAGEMENT STYLE

Take a moment for you and your mentee to visit either one of these websites and assess your conflict resolution style:

Module 3: Responses to Conflict
http://p2001.health.org/CTW06/mod3tr.htm OR

Conflict Handling Styles
http://www.pao.gov.ab.ca/toolkit/tools/conflict-handling-styles.htm.

The purpose of this exercise is to assist you and your mentee to:

♦ Identify your own preferred style(s) for dealing with conflict.

♦ Analyze how different styles might be more appropriate in various team and classroom situations.

♦ Compare and discuss your styles in the mentoring relationship.

CONFRONTING PROBLEMS

Collaborative problem solving means is that there are times when it makes sense for people who have a problem to sit down together to see if they can solve it by talking about their mutual concerns. The Office of Dispute Resolution (2004) suggests that people who are in conflict with each other often have common goals. "In the workplace, for example, common interests include: (1) the overall success of the organization, (2) communication and team-work, (3) professional competence for everyone, (4) both quality and productivity, (5) ethical treatment, and (6) recognition of our diversity." The challenge becomes finding ways to address conflicting perspectives on how these goals and interests can be met for all concerned.

Gordon (1991) tells us that one of the "mentor's primary functions is to help beginner teachers solve problems they are bound to experience" during any induction phase (p. 36). Problem solving in the current literature has been described as a process involving six key steps:

♦ Identifying and defining the problem

♦ Gathering information to determine the extent of the problem

♦ Generating possible solutions

♦ Designing an action plan to address the problem

♦ Implementing the plan

♦ Assessing the plan and revising

We strongly urge that, during the first few days of the field experience or the teaching year, you present a process to implement when either participant feels a problem has developed. This process should be discussed and mutually agreed on as a positive way to resolve any differences. We also recommend that you initiate a simulation in which you and the mentee practice these skills. The conference might look like this:

COMPETENCY 2.5: PROBLEM-SOLVING CONFERENCE GUIDE

Conference Opening

♦ Set the Tone

Example: Meet in a nonthreatening place and begin the conference by saying, "Jane, I asked to meet with you today to discuss your classroom management skills. I want to discuss two areas of concern with you and work something out that we're both comfortable with."

♦ Set the Agenda

We have 30 minutes for our discussion in which I plan to address these points: a) _____ b) _____ and c) _____

♦ Make Adjustments

Is there anything you would like to add to this agenda?

Conference Content

(Use the following questions to help guide the development of your conference. Jot down responses to help you restate important points.)

♦ Problem Reflection

• What are the signs of the problem?

• How is the problem defined by the mentee, mentor, or supervisor?

♦ Underlying Causes

• What are the facts?

• What additional information is needed?

• What are the feelings and opinions of those involved?

• What assumptions have been made?

• Is there any inaccurate information?

- Are there any communication problems?
- What is the basic cause/reason for this problem?

♦ Desired Results

- What are the desired results of those involved?
- What are the positive aspects of this problem?

♦ Searching for a Solution/Plan of Action

- What are some promising solutions to this problem?
- What are the possible consequences for solutions generated?
- Which solution will eliminate or significantly reduce the problem being addressed?
- Select the best solution.

♦ Implementing the Solution

- Is an action plan needed?
- Develop the plan.
- How and when will the plan be evaluated?
- How will success be rewarded/recognized?
- What check points should be considered?

Conference Closing

♦ Review the problem statement

♦ Check for understanding

♦ Set direction

Collaborative problem solving is an effective way to deal with conflict. Successful negotiation engages all stakeholders in seeking ways to find a mutually satisfying solution for everyone involved. One way to minimize conflict is to identify potential problem areas. Gordon (1991) gives us a questionnaire that may be helpful in heading off potential problems before they get too serious. Helping novices to confront areas of concern brings needed information to the surface.

COMPETENCY 2.6: NEEDS ASSESSMENT FOR BEGINNING TEACHERS

Please choose the response for each item that most nearly indicates your level of need for assistance in the area described in the item.

Possible Responses:

A. Little or no need for assistance
B. Some need for assistance
C. Moderate need for assistance
D. High need for assistance
E. Very high need

_____ Finding out what is expected of me as a teacher
_____ Communicating with the principal
_____ Communicating with other teachers
_____ Communicating with parents
_____ Organizing and managing my classroom
_____ Maintaining student discipline
_____ Obtaining instructional resources/materials
_____ Planning for instruction
_____ Managing my time
_____ Diagnosing student needs
_____ Evaluating student progress
_____ Motivating students
_____ Assisting students with special needs
_____ Dealing with individual differences among students
_____ Understanding the curriculum
_____ Completing administrative paperwork
_____ Using a variety of teaching methods
_____ Facilitating group discussions
_____ Grouping for instruction
_____ Administering standardized tests
_____ Understanding the school system's teacher-evaluation process
_____ Understanding my legal rights and responsibilities
_____ Dealing with stress
_____ Dealing with union-related issues
_____ Becoming aware of special services provided by the school district

Reprinted with permission from Gordon, S. (1991). *How to help beginning teachers succeed.* Alexandria, VA: Association for Supervision and Curriculum Development, p. 43.

Prevention is the best tactical approach in resolving problems. If you can help interns and first-year teachers identify potential trouble spots, then you can assist beginners in viewing the process as a starting place for increasing their skills as decision-makers and problem solvers.

SUMMARY

"Cooperation is spelled with two letters—WE!"

V. Estrem, 1993

Effective mentors know that people skills are very important skills in the mentoring process. By taking the time to build a give-and-take relationship, you set the stage to achieve these goals:

- ◆ Increasing understanding and mutual respect.

- ◆ Acknowledging the needs and feelings of mentees.

- ◆ Focusing on the positive aspect of conflict resolution and problem solving.

- ◆ Valuing differences of others.

- ◆ Establishing a collaborative setting for fostering personal and professional growth in colleagues through systematic planning. See Appendix page 178 for a planning calendar of mentoring tasks.

REFERENCES

Black, A., & L. Davern. (1998). When a preservice teacher meets the classroom team. *Educational Leadership*, 55(5), 52–55.

Bolten, R. (1986). *People skills*. New York: Simon and Schuster.

Boreen, J., & D. Niday. (2003). *Mentoring across boundaries: Helping beginning teachers succeed in challenging situations*. Portland, MA: Stenhouse Publishers.

Chase, B. (1998). NEA's role: Cultivating teacher professionalism. *Educational Leadership*, 55(5), 18–20.

Conflict Handling Styles. (2005). From *Organizational Behavior* by Hellriegel, Slocum, Woodman, and Bruning. Reprinted with permission of ITP Nelson. Retrieved May 2006 from http://www.pao.gov.ab.ca/toolkit/tools/conflict-handling-styles.htm

Danielson, C. (1996). *Enhancing professional practice: A framework for teaching*. Alexandria, VA: Association for Supervision and Curriculum Development.

Darling-Hammond, L. (1998). Teacher learning that supports student learning. *Educational Leadership*, 55(5), 66–11.

Gordon, S. (1991). *How to help beginning teachers succeed.* Alexandria, VA: Association for Supervision and Curriculum Development.

Gordon, T. (1970). *Parent effectiveness training: The no-lose program for raising responsible children.* New York: Peter Wyden.

Heathfield, S.(2002). *Fight for what's right: Ten tips to encourage meaningful conflict.* Retrieved May 6, 2006 from http://www.human resources About.com/library/ weekly/nosearch/naa071002a.htm

Johnson, S., & S. Kardos. (2005). Bridging the generation gap. *Educational Leadership,* 62(8), 8–14.

Jonson, K. (2002). *Being an effective mentor: How to help beginning teachers succeed.* Thousand Oaks, CA: Corwin Press Inc.

Module 3: Responses to conflict. (2001). Retrieved on May 6, 2006 from p2001.health.org/ CTW06/mod3tr.htm

Office of Dispute Resolution. (2006). *A four step way of dealing with conflict.* Retrieved May 6, 2006 from, http://www1.va.gov/adr/page.cfm?pg=42#introduction

COACHING BOOSTERS

Can Teach. (2006). *Conflict resolution workshop* (for teachers). Retrieved May 6, 2006 from http://www.canteach.ca/elementary/fnations61.html

Conflict Resolution Network. (2006). *Conflict checklist.* Retrieved May 6, 2006 from http://www.crnhq.org

Kestner, P., & L. Ray. (2002). *Conflict resolution training program.* San Francisco, CA: Jossey-Bass.

Portner, H. (2002). *Being mentored: A guide for protégés.* Thousand Oaks, CA: Corwin Press, Inc.

COMPETENCY 3

NURTURING THE NOVICE: ACTIVATE COGNITIVE COACHING

COMPETENCY STATEMENT

Intensify school-based teacher induction and collegial support to accelerate and ensure the development of beginning teachers from novice to expert teaching.

KNOWLEDGE BASE HIGHLIGHTS

♦ *Boreen & Niday, 2003: "Some beginners may not be ready for self-mentoring until their second, third, or fourth year. The process typically requires teachers to recognize that they can think through appropriate responses. This inward dialogue requires critical and creative thinking skills."*

♦ *Costa & Garmston, 2002: "The mission and goal of cognitive coaching is to develop self- directedness in others." This is achieved by assisting others to enhance their capacity as a mediator of their own thinking.*

♦ *Pattersen, 2005*: "As professionals, we owe it to one another to improve the way we treat our newest and most vulnerable colleagues....Why are our least experienced teachers disproportionately assigned to teach the neediest and most difficult students?"

♦ *Lipton & Wellman, 2003*: "Effective mentors make their self-talk overt and explicit when conversing with novices. They share the concepts/standards they use for teaching decisions made, the connections they make, and the techniques they use to perceive and frame issues and problems....Skillful mentors mediate the thinking of novices and prompt reflection by inviting them to notice and analyze their patterns of thinking and problem solving."

According to Wayne, Youngs, & Fleischman (2005), "if you had asked a group of teachers in 1990 whether they received mentoring or participated in an induction program about half of them would have said yes." By 2000, the proportion had jumped to about four out of five based on research data on the impact of induction and mentoring on retaining beginning teachers (Smith & Ingersoll, 2004).

The current issue raised by researchers is how comprehensive are these induction programs? According to the Alliance for Excellent Education (2004), fewer than 1 percent qualify as delivering a comprehensive induction program that contains the following components:

♦ Reduced number of course preparations

♦ A mentor in the assigned teaching field

♦ Seminars tailored to the needs of beginning teachers

♦ Strong communication with school leaders

♦ Time for planning and collaborating with colleagues

Experts (Shields et al., 2004; Podsen, 2002; Andersen & Pellicer, 2001) claim that induction and mentoring programs can accelerate the process of helping beginning teachers to improve their teaching skills during the first three years, provided such programs offer training targeted to their adult and teacher development needs.

The career path, encumbered with environmental risks both from within the profession and the conditions of schools as a workplace, contributes to more than a 30 percent attrition rate for novices (Ingersoll & Smith, 2003). This training module focuses our attention on ways to nurture mentees in a manner that will (1) help ease the way for novices into the teaching profession; and (2) suggest ways for mentors to move mentees to more independent and expert levels of teaching through systematic cognitive coaching.

SEQUENCING THE TEACHING EXPERIENCES
FOR STUDENT INTERNS

Unlike our well-intentioned cooperating teacher, Lori, at the beginning of this book (see the Scenario One on page 1), we think you must gradually increase the intern's work responsibilities during the field experience. For example, if the field experience lasts four weeks, you might model how you perform homeroom tasks, start class, go to lunch, or work with a small group of students, asking the student intern to take notes and formulate questions. After you check for understanding, you then allow the intern to conduct these activities under your supervision. Before proceeding to more complex teaching tasks, provide feedback and more opportunities to practice. This approach does several things. First, this helps the intern to clarify what is expected beyond the realm of just teaching a lesson. Second, it gives you an opportunity to assess the ability of the intern to manage and conduct the class. It also gives you the opportunity to observe the intern's interactions with different classes to see which class will provide the best chemistry for the teaching yet to come.

We suggest that student interns be matched with classes that allow them to demonstrate their teaching skills to the best of their ability. This doesn't mean that they should not be exposed to large classes, more difficult students, and the duties of teaching; it does mean that we should sequence their field experience so that as they develop their skills they are exposed to more complex situations when they are capable of dealing with them.

For First-Year Teachers

We recommend that principals ensure that beginning teachers do not have the worst classes or more than two course preparations. We also think extra duties and professional responsibilities should be minimized during the first year until the new teacher has a firm handle on instructional preparation and classroom management. Wasley (1999) suggests that "new teachers need help with planning for a week, a month, and a year; moving kids from one activity to the next; incorporating children with disabilities or language differences; writing newsletters to parents from a culture different from the teacher's; and focusing lessons on skill acquisition and content knowledge" (p. 12). A final consideration is the location of the classroom. Whenever possible a new teacher should not be physically isolated in a remote section of the school or stationed in a trailer. If we want novices to be successful, we must at least establish the conditions that will build success rather than create obstacles.

Gordon (1991) points out that many beginning teachers left on their own view seeking help as an admission of failure and incompetence and try to cover up serious problems. Just because we may have experienced the "rites of passage" alone and unassisted doesn't mean it has to continue. By promoting favorable conditions and organizing professional duties into manageable segments, we can create a learning climate that is built on successes rather than unsuccessful attempts.

Reality Therapy

For Student Interns

Be prepared for a good dose of reality shock to set in. The majority of student interns are young adults, ranging in ages from 20 to 24, living on campus or away from home. Then suddenly the demands of real teaching consume their time and energy. They feel they are no longer in control of their lives as they spend time in a wide range of noninstructional duties, longer nights planning lessons, and frustrating days trying to keep order while they teach. For many interns, the gap between the ideal world they dreamed about and the realities of teaching cause serious doubts about their ability to be an effective teacher.

Your job as cooperating teacher mentors is to prepare them for these emotional roller coasters so that they complete their training without having a nervous breakdown. One way is to assist the intern in writing personal goals that are achievable within the field experience timeline. As we suggested earlier, planning for success through weekly conference sessions helps minimize the personal stress student interns encounter.

FOR FIRST-YEAR TEACHERS

Similarly for beginning teachers, the time demands required in lesson planning, noninstructional duties, and preparing teaching materials comes as a sudden wake-up call. For most new teachers the social isolation is overwhelming as beginners are most often expected to hit the ground running, but without much help. Peer mentors need to help first-year teachers know what is expected of them as professionals and faculty members and how to meet those expectations. By sharing the "shortcuts" to creating learning materials, planning lessons, and handling the paperwork, peer mentors can reduce job stress and help their mentees prioritize their schedules to focus more time on essential teaching tasks and less time on extraneous activities.

PROVIDING CONSTRUCTIVE FEEDBACK

This is the part that often is most difficult for cooperating teachers and peer mentors. It's easy to tell someone he or she is doing a terrific job, but communicating negative feedback constructively can be troublesome. How you deliver the "bad news" can make the difference between a novice whose performance continues to falter and one whose performance steadily rises. In his book *Freedom to Learn for the 80s,* Carl Rogers discusses the relationship between teachers and students in the classroom and how this relationship affects learning (Rogers, 1983). We can apply his principles to the mentor-mentee relationship.

Rogers tells us that the "primary task of the teacher is to permit the student to learn, to feed his or her own curiosity. Merely to absorb facts is of only slight value in the present, and is usually of even less value, now and in the future....In true teaching there is no place for the authoritarian, nor the person who is on an ego trip" (p. 18). The mentor must balance the task of allowing the novice to stretch developmentally by implementing lesson ideas, managing student behavior, and teaching the content under the mentor's watchful eye, with careful guidance, corrective feedback, and continuous support.

Unlike the role of peer mentor, the role of the cooperating teacher mentor is dual: he or she must assess the potential of the student intern as required by the university program and also assume the role of a caregiver or nurturer. Halford (1998) clearly states that the primary role of the cooperating teacher should be support provider, not formal evaluator. "Simply put, new teachers need somebody to talk to" (p. 35).

This role conflict between evaluator and nurturer is a familiar one in the clinical supervision literature. However, like professionals in other fields, teachers may need to have more direct input in the quality of the professionals who will be their teammates in the near future. For example, under the terms of the contract between the school and NEA's local affiliate in Columbus, Ohio, "the union local designates more than two dozen outstanding educators to act as full-time consulting teachers. One of these consulting teachers is assigned to every newly hired teacher. The consultants provide intensive mentoring to newcomers, and have major say in whether a newcomer is retained" (Chase, 1998, p. 20).

WHAT YOU NEED TO KNOW ABOUT ADULT LEARNING AND TEACHER DEVELOPMENT

Studies about adult development center around two themes. The first area of study looks at how adults develop their thinking processes, concept formation, and ego development. For example, as adults age, they generally reveal an improvement in their ability to relate new information to old and to make comparisons between themselves and others. The second area focuses on transitions through the life cycle and their impact on adults as they move through them. For example, adults generally move through a life span that begins with initial feelings of omnipotence, gradually shifts to stages of greater reflection and reordering of reality, and finally moves to consolidation and acceptance of life.

Glickman (1990) tells us that young adults (20–35) are usually characterized by limited experiences, simple standards of reasoning about concepts, egocentricity, and dependence on authority during a time of unlimited aspirations and feelings of power. The middle-aged adult (35–55) has acquired a vast array of experiences, has developed the ability to draw relationships between self and others, and possesses an awareness of his or her strengths and weaknesses. This stage includes a time of reexamination of one's abilities and a revision of priorities. Finally, the older adult (55+) has had numerous experiences, can understand more easily the situations of others, and can make decisions that take into account more of the total situation. At this time in life, the older adult accepts himself or herself and focuses on those activities that are most important.

Glickman (1990) provides us with an instructive discussion about the impact of conceptual development and transitions of teachers as it relates to teacher development. He contends that, similar to the general adult population, the majority of teachers appear to be operating at relatively moderate to low stages of conceptual development. This means that thought is viewed as absolute and concrete with a high dependence on authority. This would be acceptable if teaching was a simple activity and required limited need for decision making. However, we know a teacher faces more than 100 students of varying backgrounds and ability levels and must make hundreds of decisions on a daily basis. "Concrete, rigid thinking on the part of the teacher cannot possibly improve instruction....Teacher improvement can only come from abstract, multi-informational thought that can generate new responses toward new situations" (p. 54).

So what does all this mean as far as mentoring a novice? It means that part of the mentoring process is designing the teaching experience so that it fosters ways to improve thinking by asking interns to think "abstractly and act autonomously." It does not mean making the teaching situation less complex by disregarding differences among students, by establishing routines and instructional practices that remain the same day after day and year after year, and by omitting time to reflect on practice to explore new ways for teaching students (Glickman, 1990). Thinking improves when teachers interact with one another, when they experiment with novel teaching strategies, when they involve themselves in peer coaching at work, and when they assess and revise their actions. Schools traditionally have not been places where teachers have been supported in ways to improve their thinking, according to Glickman.

We know novices are concerned about survival. We understand this perspective because of their place in the life cycle. As a rule, young teachers have limited experiences to identify with and want very much to be successful. We can help to reduce fears of failure and to increase feelings of security by sequencing their experiences from simple to more complex, giving timely feedback, and probing their thought processes to ensure the development of reflective thinking skills.

WHAT YOU NEED TO KNOW ABOUT COGNITIVE COACHING

Likewise the goal of being a masterful mentor is to consciously move your mentee from dependent problem-solvers to independent, more skilled problem-solvers. Teaching is a very complex activity requiring advanced ability to think abstractly and take appropriate independent or collaborative action based on sound problem analysis, critical data collection and analysis, and creative solutions. Moving up the conceptual continuum from lower levels to higher levels of critical thinking becomes the mental exercise that mentors must infuse in their daily interactions with mentees. We think that developing your cognitive coaching skills will assist you in designing a much needed and challenging critical thinking program for coaching both experienced and novice teachers.

Glickman (2004, 1990) asserts that schools traditionally have not been places where teachers have been supported and nurtured to improve collaborative action and their critical thinking skills. Lipton and Wellman (2003) tell us that "support alone will not promote growth and learning for novice teachers. It must be balanced with learning challenges that stretch and strengthen beginner's capacities for profession thinking. Skillful mentors engage novices in structured planning, reflecting, and problem-solving conversations on a regular basis" (p. 1.3). These conversations are intended to expand mentees' scope and depth of thinking to consider deeper connections, seek root causes, and project far reaching alternatives and solutions to current problems and concerns in their teaching performances.

COGNITIVE COACHING DEFINED

Cognitive coaching is based on the idea that metacognition—or being aware of one's own thinking processes—fosters independence in learning. By providing personal insights into the learner's own thinking processes, cognitive coaching builds flexible, confident problem-solving skills. Plus, it encourages self-efficacy and pride. (Costa & Garmon, 2002).

The Center for Collaborative Support (CCS) defines cognitive coaching as a configuration that "provides all educators with clear frameworks, common language and skills to support colleagues and students in a variety of growth-producing settings. It is a way of thinking and communicating which:

♦ Enhances understanding and higher level thinking

♦ Helps others become their own problem-solvers

♦ Creates collaborative rather than dependent relationships

♦ Develops genuine trust and rapport

♦ Supports others in feeling competent in challenging work environments"

KEY PRINCIPLES AND BASIC ASSUMPTIONS

According to Barrett (1995) "the guiding principle of cognitive coaching is that instructional behaviors will not be altered until the inner thought processes of teachers are altered and rearranged" (p. 51). The mentoring process is about developing a personal relationships with colleagues for the purpose of professional instruction and guidance. As these relationships develop, astute mentors must be able to match their support to the novice's cognitive and teacher development stage.

Earlier we discussed that new teachers who solve problems at a concrete level will require more structured and frequent feedback than novices who solve problems at a more abstract, higher order level. Over time it is expected that novices will begin to solve problems similar to experts in the profession, namely their mentors. Lipton and Wellman (2003) give us three basic assumptions about the mentoring process:

1. Effective mentors consciously move their mentees from dependent problem-solvers to independent, more skilled problem-solvers.

2. Reflective questioning is the catalyst for guiding expertise in problem solving.

3. Cognitive coaching serves as the approach that assists in the transition from novice to expert teacher.

ASSUMPTION #1

Effective mentors are those who consciously move their mentees from dependent problem-solvers to autonomous, more skilled problem-solvers. The mentoring process is not stagnate, but a dynamic process in which both mentors and mentees move through various stages. Barnett (1995) summarizes these stages as:

♦ Initiation into the profession and school culture

♦ Knowledge and skill development

♦ Disillusionment at certain phases

♦ Separation from the mentor

♦ Status as a peer colleague

A healthy mentoring relationship is one that produces a more skilled and self-reliant mentee who matures into a confident peer and competent colleague. This transition is achieved when mentors carefully assess where they are in the mentoring process and select and apply specific mentoring strategies to guide the progression.

ASSUMPTION #2

Reflection is the catalyst for developing expertise in problem-solving about teaching and learning. "Reflective questioning creates opportunities for individuals to reflect aloud, to be heard by one or more colleagues, and to be prompted to expand and extend one's thinking through follow-up questions" (Lee & Barnett, 1994, p. 22). Mentors hold the key novices need to unlock their professional expertise. By demonstrating the qualities of a cognitive coach, mentors become the agents for developing expertise in reflective thinking, conceptual development, and problem-solving processes.

Lipton and Wellman (2003) assert that" expertise results from both internal and external mediation" (p. 1.8). They conclude that the self-talk of expert teachers differs significantly from that of novices. Expert teachers have extensive repertoires for all of the major teaching tasks. These preestablished patterns and procedures free their attention for more focused student-centered interactions and responses. Novices, however, tend to view and respond to discrete teaching behaviors and events in isolation. When novices observe expert teachers they are amazed at the automatic responses and seamless interactions with students. Without the self-talk and explanation of the mentor following these observations, the teaching performance remains a mystery to the novice. Therefore, it becomes essential that mentors be able to clarify and explain their teaching behaviors both informally and formally.

ASSUMPTION #3

Cognitive coaching serves as the approach that assists in this transition from novice to expert teacher. If teachers are going to increase their impact on student learning, the research suggests that on-going professional development is essential. On the job experiences by itself will not produce expertise. The professional literature emphasizes that novices need to receive adequate instruction and be actively engaged with professionals who can model expert reflective thinking about their teaching (Lipton & Wellman,

2003; Costa & Garmon, 2002; Barrett, 1995). In particular, early level teachers need to expand their content knowledge and pedagogical skills within their subject area specialization. "It is a teacher's professional responsibility to examine, refine, and broaden his or her practice on a continuing basis" (McColsky & Egelson, 1993, p. 382). But in order to do this, a culture of continuous cognitive reflection on curriculum and instruction must be valued and embedded in the professional learning community.

COGNITIVE COACHING TOOLS

To help facilitate the cognitive coaching process, mentors need to be well versed in strategic cognitive coaching skills. Practicing and applying these skills will assist you in developing your ability to be an effective cognitive coach which will result in the following outcomes:

♦ Build your confidence in establishing collegial relationships, trust and rapport.

♦ Increase your skill in conducting high level planning, reflecting and problem-solving conversations.

♦ Promote your ability to create and ask questions which lead to higher level thinking.

♦ Focus your mentoring conversations with greater purpose, impact and understanding.

Cognitive coaching uses the techniques of active listening, pausing, paraphrasing, and questioning to help colleagues to think about their thinking. These skills are not new to you but the question becomes how consciously and consistently do you use them. In *Competency 2: Promoting Collaborative Learning,* you were asked to take a Communication Inventory (p. 61). Review your responses to questions 4, 5, and 6. Part of fostering a trusting relationship is evidenced by (1) active listening skills, (2) positive rapport and (3) inviting verbal behaviors.

ACTIVE LISTENING SKILLS

Think for a minute about your conversations with your colleagues and even your students. How would you characterize the communication between you? Who does most of the talking? Often when people talk to each other, they don't listen attentively. They are often distracted, half listening, half thinking about something else. How would you describe your ability to listen fully and attentively?

Now think about a person who has influenced you or an individual whom you feel really knows and understands you. Who does most of talking in these conversations? In one-to-one relationships with someone who knows us well, the communication flows between us effortlessly. We really feel connected and understood. Does this happen because we excel at expressing ourselves, or because we are masters of listening?

We know both aspects are important, but, to coin a phrase, talk is cheap and listening is rare. Chances are that those who influence us most are expert listeners.

Whether instinctively or through practice, expert listeners demonstrate their powerful skills as empathetic and active listeners. A University of Maine researcher, Dr. Marisue Pickering (1986), identifies four characteristics of empathetic listeners. The desire to:

1. Be other-directed, rather than to project one's own feelings and ideas onto the other.

2. Be nondefensive, rather than to protect the self.

3. Imagine the roles, perspectives, or experiences of the other, rather than assuming they are the same as one's own.

4. Listen as a receiver, not as a critic, and desire to understand the other person rather than to achieve either agreement from or change in that person.

BUILDING RAPPORT

Rapport might be defined as the ability to make a personal connection and show empathy. The professional literature suggests rapport is fostered through both verbal and non-verbal components. Verbal aspects include such factors as the pitch, volume, and inflection we use in our voice patterns, and the general pacing of our conversations. Nonverbal aspects include such factors as our body posture, use of gestures, proximity to our peer partner, eye contact and our facial expressions. While these are all important characteristics, we will not delve into these areas. There are extensive resources that can provide more information and checklists for you to use if you want to assess your skills related to these topics (e.g., *Top Ten Body Language Tips* available at: http://www.selfgroeth.com/articles/phipps3.html).

LINGUISTIC SKILLS

Active listening is a structured form of listening and responding that focuses the attention on the speaker. You as the mentor/listener must take care to attend to the mentee fully, and then paraphrase what he or she thinks the mentee has said. You do not have to agree with the mentee—you must simply state what you think the mentee said. This enables the mentee to find out whether or not you have really understood their concern or dilemma. If you did not fully capture the real meaning expressed by the mentee, you can then generate specific clarifying questions and the mentee can respond in more detail.

The behaviors associated with linguistic ability are (1) pausing and using silence, (2) paraphrasing and (3) mediational questioning (Lipton & Wellman, 2003; Costa & Garmon, 2002).

PAUSES AND USE OF SILENCE

This skill provides time for you to think about the speaker's message and frame a response. It is most like wait time you apply with your students so they can think about their answers before you call on anyone to respond.

PARAPHRASES

This skill signals active listening on your part and attention to the speaker. There are two types you might want to use:

> *Type 1—Acknowledge/Clarify:* In this paraphrase type you acknowledge feelings or clarify content expressed; e.g., "It sounds like you are very frustrated….It seems that you are saying…."

> *Type 2—Summarize/Organize:* In this paraphrase type you separate confusing or multiple issues expressed; e.g., "You have described several ideas related to….You seem most concerned about…."

COMPETENCY 3.1.
PARAPHRASE PRACTICE

Read each of the speaker statements and create a paraphrase for each type.

Speaker's Statement:

"I am really having a difficult time teaching this class. The range in their ability levels are too broad and I find myself planning for 30 different lessons!"

Acknowledge/Clarify	Summarize/Organize

Speaker's Statement:

"I don't see how I can prepare my students to meet the state's new performance standards. They have below grade level reading skills and their attitudes toward school are poor. And on top of this we are required to teach them social and academic skills!"

Acknowledge/Clarify	Summarize/Organize

MEDIATIONAL QUESTIONS

This skill helps you to move the mentee along the critical thinking continuum by shifting their level of abstract thinking from concrete levels to more abstract levels. Mediational questioning will assist in developing your colleagues awareness of their own cognitive processes and their intellectual pathways. Here are three categories for you to explore:

- *Clarifying Questions* will help you to seek more information on the ideas expressed, discover the meaning of the language used, determine the reasons for decisions made or proposed, or seek connections to important issues and standards. For example: Would you tell me a little more about...? So when you say...are you suggesting...? Tell me what you mean when you...? To what extent do these strategies link to...?

- *Probing Questions* will help you to focus your mentee's thinking by reducing vague references to students, situations, and standards. For example:

   Mentee: I want my students to understand these ideas.

   Cognitive Coach: When you say understand, what specifically do you want your students to be able to do?

   Mentee: My students behaved better today.

   Cognitive Coach: In what ways were they better? What benchmarks did they meet?

- *Inquiring Questions* will help you to challenge your mentee to expand their thinking processes by analyzing, synthesizing and evaluating their teaching behaviors. For example:

Hypothesize	What's another way you might...?
Analyze	What best practices were evident in the...?
Imagine	What would it look like if...?
Compare and Contrast	How was ...different from/like...?
Extrapolate	How could this...be applied in...?
Evaluate	What sort of impact did...have on...?

Competency 3.2.
Mediational Questions Practice

Read the speaker's statement and develop questions to promote higher level thinking.

Speaker's Statement:

"My third period class is getting more out of control. I have tried everything to settle them down and keep them more on task."

Clarifying Questions	Probing Questions	Inquiry Questions

SENSITIVITY TO THE NOVICE'S TEACHER-PREPARATION PROGRAM

Part of nurturing beginners is finding ways to build on their previous learning. A good way to do this is to find out more about their program of study. Generally, teacher-education programs have student-teaching handbooks, and some may have guides for mentor teachers. Ask your mentee to bring these items to you. A quick review of these types of materials may prove valuable in sizing up your mentee's education and training. They certainly will acquaint you with the teacher-education program's philosophy and expected program outcomes. We know your time is precious, but acquiring insight into these matters may help you understand where the novice is coming from and what the teacher-education program expects. Bridging the communication gap between training institutions and the local schools can only help the process to work more effectively.

COLLABORATING WITH SUPERVISORS

FOR STUDENT INTERNS

When you begin developing a plan of action as suggested in "Competency 2: Promoting Collaborative Learning," be sure to include the college supervisor. Most field supervisors don't want to overload you with lengthy conferences or conversations, especially during a busy day, but there should be a plan in place to communicate with the college supervisor how things are going and what the supervisor can do to help you and the intern. Generally, the field supervisor will make weekly visits and observations, depending on the nature of the internship. Communication is enhanced when assessments are shared with all participants present. E-mail may be a very effective tool for you to use as a way to alert the supervisor of any potential problems or a means to exchange needed information about the intern.

FOR FIRST-YEAR TEACHERS

Formal evaluation by the members of the administrative team can be very intimidating to a first-year teacher. Peer mentors can help to reduce anxiety by preparing mentees for the required observations and communicating with department chairs and principals about the readiness of their mentees for a formal evaluation. First visits might be announced so that peer mentors can help first-year teachers prepare both technically and emotionally.

SUMMARY

"The ultimate measure of a man is not where he stands in moments of comfort and convenience, but where he stands at times of challenge and controversy."

Martin Luther King Jr.
(V. Caruana, 1998)

In this module, we examined your role in providing a supportive setting in which to mentor a novice. We began by asking you to think about ways to sequence the teaching experience in order to build skills in a systematic manner. We know that no one can learn for another; mentees must do it for themselves. However, similar to the way we organize learning of content and skills for students, we need to organize the process, model effective techniques, and offer constructive counsel to help beginners do something they cannot yet do. We also asked you to consider how schools could organize the workplace to make the conditions more favorable for first-year success. Learning more about how adults learn and how life transitions affect adult development will assist you in designing teaching experiences based on the age, maturity, life experiences, and level of conceptual functioning of your mentee. Finally, we encouraged you to learn more about the novice's teacher-preparation program and develop your cognitive coaching skills to help find ways to build on previous learning and contemporary views of teaching and learning.

REFERENCES

Alliance for Excellent Education. (2004). *Tapping the potential: Retaining and developing high quality new teachers.* Washington, DC: Author.

Anderson, L., & L. Pellicer. (2001). *Teacher peer assistance and review: A practical guide for teachers and administrators.* Thousand Oaks, CA: Corwin Press.

Barnett, B. (1995). Developing reflection and expertise: Can mentors make the difference? *Journal of Educational Administration*, 33(5), 45–59.

Boreen, J., & D. Niday. (2003). *Mentoring across boundaries: Helping beginning teachers succeed in challenging situations*. Portland, MA: Stenhouse Publishers.

Chase, B. (1998). NEA's role: Cultivating teacher professionalism. *Educational Leadership*, 55(5), 18–20.

Center for Collaborative Support (nd) *Cognitive coaching*. Retrieved May 17, 2006 from http://www.snoqualmie.k12.wa.us/Center%20for%20Collaborative%20Support _files/Cognitive%20Coaching.asp

Costa, A., & R. Garmston. (2002). *Cognitive coaching: Implementation guide*. Sandy, UT: LPD Video Journal of Education and TeachStream.

Delgado, M. (1999). Lifesaving 101: How a veteran teacher can help a beginner. *Educational Leadership*, 56(8), 27–29.

Glickman, C. (2004). *SuperVision and instructional leadership*, 6th ed. Boston: Allyn and Bacon.

Glickman, C. (1990). *Supervision of instruction*. Boston: Allyn and Bacon.

Gordon, S. (1991). *How to help beginning teachers succeed*. Alexandria, VA: Association for Supervision and Curriculum Development.

Halford, J. (1998). Easing the way for new teachers. *Educational Leadership*, 55 (5), 33–36.

Ingersoll, R.M., & T.M. Smith. (2004). The wrong solution to the teacher shortage. *Educational Leadership*, 60 (8), 30–33.

Lee, G. & Barnett, B. (1994). Using reflective questioning to promote collaborative dialogue. *Journal of Staff Development* (Winter 1994), 22–27.

Lipton, L & B. Wellman. (2003). *Making mentoring work*. Alexandria, VA: Association for Supervision and Curriculum Development.

McColskey, W., and Egelson, P. (1993). *Designing teacher evaluation systems that support professional growth*. Greensboro, NC: Southeastern Regional Vision for Education, School of Education, University of North Carolina at Greensboro. (ERIC ED 367 662)

Pattersen, M. (2005). Hazed. *Educational Leadership*, 62 (8), 20–23.

Pickering, M. (1986). Communication in *Explorations*, A Journal of Research of the University of Maine, Vol. 3, No. 1, Fall 1986, pp 16–19. Retrieved May 2006 from, http://crs.uvm.edu/gopher/nerl/personal/comm/e.html

Podsen, I.J. (2002). *Teacher retention: What is your weakest link?* Larchmont, NY: Eye on Education.

Rogers, C. (1983). *Freedom to learn for the 80s.* New York: Macmillan.

Schields, P., Haslam, B., LaGuardia, K. et al. (2004). *Identification and description of promising models of teacher induction.* Menlo Park, CA: SRI International.

Smith, T.M., & R.M. Ingersoll (2004). What are the effects of induction and mentoring on beginning teacher turnover? *American Educational Research Journal,* 41(3), 681–714.

Wayne, A., Youngs, P., & S. Fleischman. (2005). Improving teacher induction. *Educational Leadership,* 62 (8), 76–77.

Wasley, P. (1999). Teaching worth celebrating, *Educational Leadership,* 56(8), 8–13.

COACHING BOOSTERS

Costa, A., & R. Garmston. (2002). *Cognitive coaching.* Sandy, UT: LPD Video Journal of Education and TeachStream.

Glickman, C. (2004). *SuperVision of instruction.* Boston: Allyn and Bacon. (See Chapter 4: Contrasting Optimal Adult Development with Actual Teacher Development: Clues for Supervisory Practice).

Lipton, L., & B. Wellman (2003). *Mentoring Matters: A practical guide to learning-focused relationships.* Sherman, CT: Mira Via, LLC.

COMPETENCY 4

DEVELOPING YOUR PERFORMANCE-COACHING SKILLS

COMPETENCY STATEMENT

Develop the knowledge and skills needed to enable interns and beginning teachers to perform at their highest level.

KNOWLEDGE BASE HIGHLIGHTS

♦ *Farnham-Diggory, 1994:* "Basically there are four approaches to teaching: *talking*, which centers on lecturing and questioning; *displaying*, which involves modeling and demonstrating; *coaching*, which offers cueing and guiding; and *arranging the learning environment.*"

♦ *Killian & Harrison, 2005:* "Coaches often spend time modeling instruction or observing new teachers, giving feedback on their practice, and striving to assist novices to reflect on their practice."

♦ *Lyons & Pinnell, 2001:* "Coaching is a way to help teachers become more analytic about their work" and supports them as they apply knowledge, develop skills, polish technique, and deepen their understanding."

♦ *Rowley, 1999:* "The mentor training program should equip mentors with the knowledge, skills, and dispositions prerequisite to effective coaching."

What comes to mind when you picture the tennis pro, the swimming coach, the equestrian trainer, the music teacher, or the physical education instructor working with amateurs? Probably you see trainers watching from the sidelines as the learners practice or perform certain skills. Coaches observe, assess, prompt, cajole, encourage, and demonstrate techniques and skills needed by athletes or performers to succeed. These behaviors form the basic interactions needed to successfully coach and mentor any aspiring novice.

According to Keefe and Jenkins (1997), "coaching must be directed to aspects of students' working memories—goal setting, awareness of cues, retrieval of knowledge, the actual performance, and self-monitoring" (p. 92). Similarly, to learn complex teaching tasks, interns and beginning teachers need to construct working models for these tasks. Performance coaching is aimed at building these working schemes with teacher mentors suggesting attainable goals, pointing out missed cues, showing alternative ways of performing, and providing ways for novices to critique and monitor their own performance.

PERFORMANCE COACHING— A FIVE-STEP PROCESS

Here is a prototype that articulates a five-step process to guide your development as a performance coach.

STEP 1: PRESENT THE BASIC KNOWLEDGE, OPERATING SKILLS, AND/OR RATIONALE FOR THE TEACHING SKILL

The teacher-preparation program provides the foundation or core knowledge base for aspiring teachers to integrate their content and pedagogical knowledge and skills. Beginning in the sophomore year, interns take courses related to a major in education. These courses usually include an introduction to education, human growth and development, and instructional technology. Often students are required to spend time observing schools, teachers, and students in a variety of settings. By the end of the sophomore term, students seek admission into the teacher-education program. Once admitted, first-term juniors begin the professional sequence of courses that prepares them to become competent in a particular content area, learning the methods of teaching that content and of classroom management. Throughout these courses, additional requirements in teacher-education programs include field visits to help students connect new knowledge and skills to actual job experiences. The senior year requires extended internships that are intended to immerse students into the workplace under the mentorship of an experienced and effective teacher and a college supervisor.

This information may be useful as you help interns and beginning teachers connect what they have learned to what they see in your classroom and choose to do during their early teaching experiences. The ability to conceptualize and manipulate ideas and concepts varies. You will find most interns and first-year teachers able to make the connections between theory and practice fairly quickly as they observe experienced teachers and begin to articulate their understanding; however, some interns and beginning teachers need more time to transfer the text knowledge and concepts into applicable teaching behaviors. These novices, in particular, need a structured sequencing of teaching tasks from less to more complex. In these situations, mentors may need to reteach or reinforce key concepts and skills as they apply to the current teaching situation.

STEP 2: DEMONSTRATE HOW THE SKILL WORKS UNDER VARYING CONDITIONS WITHIN CLASSROOMS

Gordon (1991) tells us that mentors and mentees are natural partners for co-teaching. He emphasizes that one advantage of co-teaching for the novice is that the beginner not only observes you, the skilled expert in action, but also is actively involved with the teaching experience as your teaching partner. Interns or first-year teachers get to see how a master teacher moves through the entire process—diagnosing student needs, setting learning objectives, planning the lesson, managing the class, and evaluating results. Novices who are co-teachers get the chance to follow your lead, plan and present parts of lessons, interact with students under limited time segments, and, in general, see, up close and personal, your lesson plans, your relationships with students, your teaching style, and your organizational processes. In return, you get to observe, question, dialogue, and coach novices as they perform under controlled and well-sequenced circumstances.

Co-teaching lends itself to building a collaborative relationship between mentees and mentors. But even more, it sets the stage for the independent practice yet to come. In particular, student interns are often left sitting passively, observing their cooperating teachers until it's time for them to teach their one-week unit or to take over a particular class. Co-teaching gives interns the chance to work side by side with a professional as they build toward the moment when they will have to take over a teaching assignment.

For first-year teachers, co-teaching reduces feelings of isolation as mentor teachers listen and dialog with mentees about how and why a particular lesson will be taught or managed and then suggest ways to reduce preparation time, prioritize instructional activities, and prevent potential problems. When peer mentors are paired with first-year teachers based on similar courses, content, and students, the mentor can organize instruction so that the mentee teaches the same lesson content a week after the mentor. In this approach, the beginner can observe the mentor teach the content and then utilize the lesson plans and the materials developed to teach the lesson with his or her students. If this matching is not possible between mentors and mentees, the mentor can ask another colleague to provide this type of assistance. This approach expands collaborative efforts among the teaching faculty and gives the first-year teacher an additional peer coach.

STEP 3: LET THE NOVICE PRACTICE THE SKILL IN NONTHREATENING CONDITIONS

During the co-teaching experience, novices get the chance to practice what you demonstrate. This process is called *modeling*. It might go like this. You introduce a particular lesson, making sure you demonstrate such things as (a) getting students' attention, (b) setting the learning objective, and (c) relating the learning to students' life experiences. The novice observes, takes notes, and prepares to do the same introduction or a similar one with the next class while you observe and take notes on what happened or didn't happen. At the first opportunity, you both discuss the performance. The novice reflects on what you did and how you did it. You now give him/her the opportunity to describe your performance. Then you observe the mentee and offer feedback, using the agreed-upon performance criteria to guide your reflection. Your notes might look like this:

Mentor Teacher A:

> Beth did a good job of settling the students. She wrote the objectives on the board. She did an excellent job getting the attention of the students and leading the discussion.

or

Mentor Teacher B:

> 9:30—Beth greeted students as they entered the class, smiling and calling many by name. She directed them to copy down the day's learning objective into their daily agendas. As students settled, Beth scanned the room to take attendance. One student came in late, and Beth quietly took his late slip.

> 9:35—She got the students' attention by asking them to jot down the television shows they watched last night and rank them from 1 (least liked) to 5 (best liked). Then she directed them to share their list with a partner and explain why they ranked a particular program least liked or best liked. Students responded enthusiastically by getting right on task.

> 9:40—Beth stated the objective for the day's lesson when she said, "Today, we are going to practice how to write a persuasive paragraph. What does the word *persuasive* mean? Tell your partner what you think the word means." She then called on several students for their definitions. Several students called out answers without raising their hand. Beth reminded them of the procedure and they complied.

> 9:45—Beth asked the students to think about the importance of being able to persuade another person to do or not do something. She conducted a five-minute discussion. Most of the students were on task. Three boys

toward the back were talking and passing notes. Beth did not notice their off-task behavior. After five minutes they stopped. Beth may need to scan the room more often during a group discussion.

STEP 4: PROVIDE FEEDBACK ON PERFORMANCE THAT IS SPECIFIC AND NONJUDGMENTAL

Which set of notes would Beth find more helpful? Why? Feedback is essential to the development of interns and beginning teachers. It not only helps novices correct mistakes before they become major headaches, but it also reinforces positive behaviors and encourages the development of effective teaching behaviors.

Effective feedback is helpful, focuses on specific changeable behavior, states the impact of the behavior clearly, and is timely (Thompson, 1996). Effective feedback includes a description of the behavior in objective and nonjudgmental terms and a suggestion of what would be more effective, especially if the behavior has a negative impact. Finally, effective feedback is well timed and provided at regular intervals. If you establish a plan at the very beginning of the mentoring experience to establish ways and mechanisms to communicate feedback, you will go a long way in fostering the notion that talking about successes and mistakes is a way to encourage responsible risk taking and professional growth.

Positive feedback can be a powerful motivator when it is specific and behavioral. Global compliments, while flattering, are too broad to be useful in identifying and maintaining effective teaching behaviors. Develop a system of looking for and recognizing specific positive behaviors. Such reinforcement will increase the confidence level of novices as well as the incidence of those behaviors.

EXERCISE 4.1. OBJECTIVE DATA COLLECTION

Ask a trusted peer if you can observe part of a class. Practice taking anecdotal notes that are specific, descriptive, and nonjudgmental. Model Mentor Teacher B. Share your notes with your colleagues for feedback. Examine your notes for any global notations; for example, *Bill did a great job with the lesson.* Look for specific positive behaviors you can reinforce; for example, *Bill showed effective skill in questioning his students and starting the discussion with low-level types of cognitive questions (recall and comprehension) and moving to higher levels (application and synthesis).*

STEP 5: EMPLOY A SYSTEMATIC COACHING CYCLE THAT INCLUDES CONFERENCES TO ENCOURAGE NOVICES TO REFLECT ON THEIR TEACHING AND DEVELOP PROBLEM-SOLVING SKILLS

Clinical supervision, according to Snyder and Anderson (1988), is a "coaching technology for improving the practice and the results of teaching" (p. 166). Coaching provides the novice with feedback on those practices that should be continued and those that should be changed, with specific evidence to back up this recommendation. The last step in the process of learning to be an effective performance coach provides the glue to hold all the discrete parts together. Clinical guidance is a way to promote systematic communication and feedback between mentors and mentees at the various stages in the mentoring process. For the best results, a systematic coaching cycle is linked to standards of teaching, to annual school improvement goals, and ultimately to summative evaluation. The five-stage process described is based on Goldhammer's clinical supervision model (Goldhammer, Anderson, & Krajewski, 1980).

Stage One:
Preobservation Conference

Purpose: To set the goals for the coaching cycle
Tasks:

- Set the logistics for the coaching cycle
- Negotiate instructional content, lesson objectives, teaching strategies
- Target instructional behaviors to be observed
- Ask mentee for feedback focus
- Establish trust and collaboration

The preobservation conference is an important first step in the cycle and an effective way to build trust and increase collaboration between mentors and mentees. This conference provides you with the opportunity to ask specific questions about the lesson, the teaching strategies selected, the assessment methods, the materials chosen or developed, the classroom management techniques, and the relationship of this lesson to previous and subsequent lessons (Glickman, 1990; Garland & Shippy, 1995). Your questions should allow the novice to reflect on decision-making processes made in planning the lesson in order to self-assess both the strengths of the lesson plan and possible problem areas. Once the novice has explained the lesson design and the "whys" of decisions made, you might make suggestions about the lesson, particularly if you note an unforeseen problem not recognized by the beginner.

The last part of the conference should center on the specific teaching behaviors you will be observing during the lesson and the selection and design of a data-collection system. Here's one sample used by a teacher mentor:

COMPETENCY 4.1: OBSERVATION FORMS

Teacher:_____

Subject: _____Date:_____

Instructional Teaching Behaviors

Presenting Instruction

Beginning the Lesson

	Very Effective	Effective	Somewhat Effective	Growth Area
• Gain attention				
• State objective				
• Establish purpose of the lesson				

Middle of the Lesson

	Very Effective	Effective	Somewhat Effective	Growth Area
• Input: Demonstrates the ability to present the content through a variety of instructional strategies such as lecture, discussion, group work, etc.; dem onstrates the ability to sequence the content logically.				
• Modeling: Demonstrates the ability to model classroom behaviors, for example, using technically correct written and oral language, courtesy, listening skills, and acceptance.				
• Guided Practice: Demonstrates the ability to break down learning into manageable steps by providing examples, demonstrations, and guided practice to ensure student understanding.				

	Very Effective	Effective	Somewhat Effective	Growth Area
• Checking for Understanding: Demonstrates the ability to monitor student understanding by seeking a variety of responses from varied students.				

Ending the Lesson

	Very Effective	Effective	Somewhat Effective	Growth Area
• Closure				
• Independent practice				
• Follow-up assignments				

Classroom Management Behaviors

	Very Effective	Effective	Somewhat Effective	Growth Target
• Communicates clear expectations about behavior				
• Distributes materials efficiently				
• Avoids unnecessary delays, interruptions, and digressions				
• Manages efficient transitions				
• Provides clear directions				
• Promotes on-task student behavior				
• Monitors behavior throughout the room				
• Intervenes appropriately when students are off-task and nondisruptive				
• Intervenes appropriately when students are off-task and disruptive to the learning of others				
• Establishes a supportive and nonthreatening learning atmosphere				

Discussion of these topics brings all the key elements to the conference table. The intern or beginning teacher by now has cotaught a lesson or a unit with you, and you have started the feedback and coaching process in the least threatening manner. Now you both are ready to formalize the process as you begin to prepare for the solo performance of the novice or the continued teaching of the beginning teacher; however; solo doesn't necessarily mean unassisted. The preobservation conference gives you another opportunity to check the novice's conceptual level of understanding of complex teaching tasks and how they apply to actual classrooms.

Glickman (1990) tells us that we can classify the abstract level of thinking of teachers as low, moderate, or high.

> Teachers with low levels of abstract thinking have difficulty in determining whether changes in classrooms are necessary. Often they do not see the relationship of their own behavior to the problem; they may say, "The students are lazy," or "The parents don't care." If they perceive a need for change, they often expect someone else to tell them exactly what to do. Left to themselves, they often respond to a dilemma by making a decision that is either habitual ("Whenever a student misbehaves, I give him more homework") or impulsive ("I changed the assignment because I felt like it") (p. 61).

Teachers with moderate levels of abstract thinking can often identify a problem but have some difficulty deciding what action to take and what the ramifications might be of certain decisions. Glickman points out that teachers at this level are "limited in determining the relationships between their teaching practices, materials, organization, and student needs" (p. 62).

At the opposite end of the continuum, highly abstract teachers can use a rational process of problem solving by incorporating several sources of information and applying their own knowledge and experiences. They can define problems beyond the surface-level symptoms, relate this information to change in classroom practice, generate alternative solutions or responses, evaluate the possible effects of each choice, and, finally, select the best response for the situation.

Your assessment of how the mentee thinks will help you decide how to structure your coaching approach. Novices at the lower end of the continuum might need more structure and direction from you throughout the mentoring experience, while those at the opposite end will appear to leave you in the dust as they fly through their teaching experiences, juggling all tasks with minimal direction and assistance.

COMPETENCY 4.2: PREOBSERVATION GUIDE

Conference Opening

♦ Set the Tone

The purpose of our conference today is to discuss your upcoming lesson.

♦ Set the Agenda

Today we will talk about these aspects of a lesson:

- How you planned the lesson
- Instructional procedures you plan to use
- What classroom management techniques you will target to manage the class during the lesson
- How the data will be collected
- The time for the postconference

♦ Adjust the Agenda

Is there anything else you would like to discuss?

Conference Content

Use the agenda to guide the conference content. Take notes on each aspect, so you can paraphrase and note suggestions made.

Conference Closing

Explain how you will collect your data, review performance criteria, and set the time and date for the postconference review.

Stage Two:
Classroom Observation and Data Collection

Purpose: To record observable patterns of teaching and learning.
Tasks:

- ♦ Record samples of behavior that relate to effective teaching behaviors
- ♦ Collect data systematically and objectively using descriptive language
- ♦ Observe for specific behaviors and their impact on the learning process

Follow the preobservation conference by observing the lesson discussed, using the observation instrument selected in the conference. We suggest you take short, objective, and descriptive notes of the performance. Brophy and Good (1974) inform us that teachers often alter teaching practices on their own after their performance has been described by an observer. If possible, incorporate videotaping; this is a strong tool for improving performance. This method allows the master teacher and the mentee to review the lesson and stop the tape at various points to reinforce strengths and problem spots in the lesson.

This, of course, is not the only way to observe classrooms. The choice of observation instrument and method depends on purpose and focus of the observation. Alternative methods include categorical frequencies, visual diagramming, space utilization, open-ended narratives, or focused questionnaires. This technique, suggesting anecdotal note-taking on specific teaching behaviors, is offered as an efficient way to get started. No matter what method you decide to use, Glickman (1990) reminds the observer to remember the difference between factual description of events and evaluative interpretations; the latter should follow your objective factual description.

Stage Three:
Analysis and Strategy

Purpose: To analyze data, identify teaching strengths and growth
              areas, and prepare for the feedback conference
Tasks:

- ♦ Review the data collected
- ♦ Relate to effective teaching research
- ♦ Identify teaching strengths and professional growth targets
- ♦ Develop the approach for the postconference session
- ♦ Outline the conference format

Once you have collected the data, you must now analyze your notes and prepare for the feedback loop in the cycle. Your task might be tallying the number of times the intern did something, or looking for patterns of behavior, or noting a significant event in the performance, or assessing which performance indicators were demonstrated and which were not. Based on specific data and concrete examples, you are now able to interpret the impact of the teaching performance. After this is done, you are better prepared to determine what interpersonal approach to use for the postobservation conference. Glickman (1990) proposes four approaches based on the abstract level of the teacher novice.

EXHIBIT 4.1. POSTOBSERVATION CONFERENCE APPROACHES

- ◆ Approach: Nondirective

  - Conference Outcome: Intern self-assesses and develops improvement plans.

  - Description

    Your role is to facilitate the novice's thinking in assessing lesson planning, presentation, and classroom management tasks. Novice develops a follow-up action plan for next lesson.

    When the conceptual level of novice is very high or the novice possess knowledge and skill, Glickman (1990) tells us to use these behaviors:
    - *Listening* until the novice completes analysis
    - *Reflecting* and paraphrasing the novice's analysis, views, and feelings
    - *Clarifying* to probe for underlying issues and understanding
    - *Encouraging* the novice to elaborate
    - *Problem solving* by asking novice to generate solutions, actions, and possible consequences of these actions

    The purpose of the nondirective conference approach is to create an active sounding board for a high-level thinker and creative professional.

- ◆ Approach: Collaborative

  - Conference Outcome: Mentor and mentee assess performance and develop improvement plans.

  - Description

    In the collaborative approach, you both share information and discuss strengths and problem areas as peers. Follow-up action is developed together.

    When the conceptual level of the novice is moderate to high, Glickman (1990) suggests you use these behaviors during the conference:
    - *Clarifying* strengths and growth areas as viewed by the novice
    - *Listening* to the novice's perspectives

- *Reflecting* and verifying the novice's perceptions of performance
- *Presenting* the mentor's point of view
- *Problem solving* mutually suggested options, negotiating differences
- *Standardizing* the plan by agreeing on the details of follow-up actions

The purpose of the collaborative approach is to develop mutual decisions and courses of action.

♦ Approach: Directive Informational

- Conference Outcome: Mentor assesses performance and suggests plan after soliciting novice's input.

- Description

In this type of conference approach, you need to provide the focus and the parameters of the lesson assessment. You allow the novice to select choices within your suggestions as you develop follow-up improvement plans.

When the conceptual level of novice is low to moderate or when the novice feels confused or at a loss of what to do, Glickman (1990) outlines these behaviors during the conference:

- *Presenting* strengths and growth areas
- *Clarifying* and asking for teacher input
- *Listening* to understand the novice's perspective
- *Problem solving* to determine possible actions
- *Directing* the alternatives
- *Asking* the novice to make a choice
- *Standardizing* the actions to be taken
- *Reinforcing* the follow-up plan

The purpose of this type of conference is to establish a clear understanding of what needs to happen to help the novice correct and or modify teaching behaviors.

♦ Approach: Directive Control

- Conference Outcome: Mentor assigns plan.

- Description

In this approach, you need to tell the novice exactly what is to be done. There are no choices offered.

When the conceptual level is low or the novice fails to show the awareness, knowledge, or desire to act on suggestions previously given to move him or her to an acceptable performance, Glickman (1990) gives us this approach:

- *Identifying* and presenting the problem (s) with the greatest negative impact on performance
- *Clarifying* the problem with the novice
- *Listening* to the novice's point of view
- *Problem solving* to seek best solution
- *Directing* specific expectations
- *Standardizing* expectations and the possible consequences for noncompliance
- *Reinforcing* and monitoring the action plan

The purpose of this type of conference is to specify what must happen to achieve an acceptable performance and clearly outline the consequences for failure to bring performance up to expectations.

Stage Four:
Postobservation Conference

Purpose: To enable the mentee to reflect on the teaching performance by identifying effective teaching behaviors and those that need improvement

Tasks:

- ◆ Establish the conference climate
- ◆ Present data
- ◆ Share interpretations
- ◆ Encourage critical thinking
- ◆ Give positive and negative feedback
- ◆ Collaborate on alternative positive behaviors
- ◆ Develop a plan for the next coaching cycle

You both come together after each has had the opportunity to reflect on the lesson. You, as the mentor, must now provide feedback that is helpful without being judgmental. According to Bolten (1986), criticizing, diagnosing, and praising in an evaluative way promote feelings of defensiveness and low self-esteem. So how do you communicate to novices needed improvements without presenting communication roadblocks? He suggests three ways:

- ◆ Describe the behavior in specific rather than fuzzy terms.
- ◆ Limit yourself to behavioral descriptions.

♦ State your description in objective terms, noting the impact of the behavior on the lesson.

If you have decided on a nondirective approach to the conference, the appropriate communication behaviors include active listening, paraphrasing, questioning, clarifying, encouraging, and reflecting. All these behaviors elicit responses from the interns that will guide them in coming up with their assessment and solutions (Shaw-Baker, 1995). Your role is to listen without making any value judgments, withhold input, verify the accuracy of solutions presented, and prompt novices to defend or support their position. We feel most interns and beginning teachers will not be at this level of thinking; however, you may have a novice who is a nontraditional student, for example, an older and more experienced adult. Sensitivity to this individual might necessitate using a more nondirective approach. Generally, as adults mature, Glickman (1990) states that "the capacity to improve and become a more integrated problem-solver exists in humans" (p. 52).

If you decide on the collaborative approach to the conference, the following communication behaviors are applicable: sharing, brainstorming, compromising, consensus, negotiating, and collaborative goal setting. We'd like to point out here that when you exercise this type of conference, you must be willing to treat interns and beginning teachers as equal partners in the process. Beginners often can present excellent ideas concerning classroom activities, classroom management techniques, and assessment strategies, but they may need assistance in formalizing the ideas into a workable plan. What follows is a sample guide using the collaborative behaviors suggested by Glickman in Exhibit 4.1 (p. 99).

COMPETENCY 4.3: POSTOBSERVATION GUIDE— COLLABORATIVE FORMAT

Conference Opening

♦ Set the Tone

The purpose of our conference today is to discuss your lesson.

♦ Set the Agenda

Today we will talk about the following aspects of the lesson:

Strengths of the lesson as they apply to:

- Planning
- Presentation
- Classroom management

Problem spots encountered as they apply to:

- Planning
- Presentation
- Classroom management

Recommendations for Improvement

♦ Adjust the Agenda

Is there anything else you would like to discuss?

Conference Content

Use the agenda to guide the conference content. Take notes on each aspect so you can paraphrase and note suggestions made. Develop the conference content based on the approach you decide is most appropriate for the intern: nondirective, collaborative, directive-informational, or directive-control. For illustration purposes, we have outlined a format for a collaborative approach.

♦ *Clarifying*: Seeking information as viewed by the intern. "Please tell me what you feel are the strengths of your lesson as it relates to planning," or "Explain to me what problems you experienced with planning the lesson."

- *Listening*: Understanding the information presented by using effective listening skills—eye contact, paraphrasing, probing, and *letting the mentee do most of the talking*. "Tell me more about how you identified the learning objectives," or "Yes, I follow your thinking process."

- *Reflecting*: Checking for understanding about the information presented. "As a summary of your strengths in the area of planning, I hear you saying...." or "Let me see if I understand the problem as you stated it....Is this your perception of the problem?"

- *Presenting*: Offering your viewpoint on the agenda items *after* the intern has presented his or her position. "Yes, I agree your planning skills are a strength area. I also noted that you included in your planning ways to manage the class during the group work part of the lesson," or "The problem as I see it relates to classroom management...."

- *Clarifying*: Making sure the intern understands your position on the topic. "Can you tell me your understanding of how I view your strengths in teaching today's lesson?" or "What do you think I am saying about...?"

- *Problem solving*: Mutually identifying solutions and options. "Let's brainstorm individually about ways to strengthen the beginning part of your lesson. Then we'll share our ideas."

- *Encouraging divergent views*: Staying open to ideas and accepting a difference of opinions. "It appears we have very different ideas about how to handle this situation. How can we come to a mutually agreeable solution? Where do we agree and where do we differ?"

Conference Closing

- Standardizing

  Mutual agreement on the follow-up action plan. "Let's fill out this action plan form to show how we will follow up on the solution we have both proposed and agreed upon."

We hope it doesn't happen often, but on occasion, you may need to take a more authoritative position to inform, direct, and assess performance. Shaw-Baker (1995) describes the communication behaviors for directive conferences as presenting, clarifying, controlling, directing, standardizing, and reinforcing. These types of conferences ask you to accurately and factually review the data collected from the observation, analyze the data and relate them to the assessment instrument, present your findings, and develop a plan of action. Your role is to make clear your expectations of what needs to happen to reach a satisfactory performance.

You may or may not experience a confrontation with the novice, but if you do here's a back-up plan to consider if things start to get argumentative. We feel your ability to understand and practice basic conflict resolution skills during these difficult conferences can help save the professional relationship. Bolten (1986) gives a three-step conflict resolution model:

1. *Treat the novice with respect.* You will need to convey an attitude of respect for the beginner, even if the individual is defensive and emotional. You can accomplish this by keeping a calm voice tone, carefully choosing your words, and sitting side by side. Your goal here is to shift the direction of the conversation from *talking at* one another to *talking with* one another.

2. *Listen until you can empathize with novice's view.* Put your active listening skills to work. You give eye contact without looking angry or upset, you reflect on the feelings and emotions that are being expressed, and you paraphrase the viewpoints of the novice showing you heard and understand his/her position.

3. *State your views, needs, and feelings.* You now get the chance to present your views of the situation and express your concerns. Again, your choice of words and tone will be important. Strive to be factual and objective, yet empathetic. When both of you have heard one another out, then it's time to mutually reach a resolution. For additional tips in managing this type of conference, refer to the problem-solving conference format that we presented in Competency 2.5 (p. 67).

EXERCISE 4.2. DESIGNING A POSTCONFERENCE GUIDE

Develop a postconference guide that reflects a nondirective approach. Use this guide in the clinical simulation suggested below. (The postconference guide presented in Competency 4.3 (p. 103), which outlines a collaborative approach, may be helpful.)

EXERCISE 4.3. CLINICAL SUPERVISION SIMULATION

Select a trusted peer and request his or her help so you can practice the five-step clinical guidance model outlined in this competency model. If possible, videotape each conference so that you can review your conference framework and interpersonal approaches. Include feedback from your peer in your self-analysis. Use the tools included in this module and begin to modify them for your professional use.

Stage Five:
Coaching Cycle Reflection

Purpose: To identify coaching strengths of the cycle and alternative behavior for mentor to improve mentoring skills

Tasks:

- ◆ Reflect on behavior patterns for each stage of the coaching cycle.

- ◆ Ask the mentee what was helpful, what might have happened differently, and what needs to happen in the next coaching cycle.

- ◆ Summarize what needs to be reinforced and what needs to be changed.

This last stage of the coaching cycle gives both mentors and mentees an opportunity to discuss the effectiveness of the mentoring process. When both parties share in the analysis, this brings to the surface behaviors that didn't work as well as expected and provides a mechanism to share concerns and reinforce effort. The ultimate goal is to increase student achievement through effective teaching performance. The coaching cycle provides a systematic way in which teacher mentors can build self-esteem while inviting novices to think and behave at higher levels of professional performance. Refer to the Appendix for suggested agendas and checklists to help you develop a timeline for your mentoring tasks (Mentoring Agenda for Cooperating Teacher, p. 179, Agenda for First-Year Teacher Mentors, p. 182; and First-Year Teacher Checklist and Reminders, p. 186).

SUMMARY

"Treat people as if they were what they ought to be and you
can help them to become what they are capable of being."

Johann Wolfgang von Goethe
(V. Caruana, 1998)

Developing your performance-coaching skills will serve you well as you work with student interns and beginning teachers. Here's what several experienced teachers said about their first mentoring experience:

In coaching and mentoring a beginning teacher, I have learned from others to take risks in my own teaching. I learned I have effective teaching skills and I can share them to help others. I also learned that I need to be open to new ideas and ways of teaching in order to keep my own teaching fresh and exciting.

I have realized that we all desire and need to learn from other teachers. That sharing positive thoughts, skills, ideas, classroom management tips is as important as sharing negatives. That peer input and suggestions are valuable resources.

Teaching is a profession that is constantly changing as new ways of thinking emerge.

Being a coach and mentor is an encouraging process, especially if those involved create a mutually respectful atmosphere. It was great to bounce off ideas and concerns as well as receive input.

It's a big responsibility, one that should be taken seriously. It provides opportunity to have a positive impact on another teacher as well as his or her students.

In being a coach and a mentor, I believe I am becoming more reflective on my own methods of teaching by asking myself questions and looking for new ways to connect with my students.

The most important factors for me in mentoring are feeling comfortable with one another, treating one another as professional equals, mutually valuing each others' input, and seeking to learn from observing one another.

Teaching can be improved when we work cooperatively with peers. Having someone observe and reflect on my teaching helps me look at what I do from a new angle.

I learned that feedback from a peer can do wonders in developing self-efficacy.

REFERENCES

Brophy, J. E., & T. L. Good (1974). *Teacher-student relationships: Causes and consequences.* New York: Holt, Rinehart and Winston.

Bolton, R. (1986). *People skills.* New York: Simon and Schuster.

Farnham-Diggory, S. (1994). Paradigms of knowledge and instruction. *Review of Educational Research, 64*(3), 463–477.

Garland, C., & V. Shippy. (1995). *Guiding clinical experiences and effective supervision in teacher education.* Norwood, NJ: Ablex.

Glickman, C. (1990). *Supervision of instruction.* Needham Heights, MA: Allyn and Bacon.

Goldhammer, R., R. Anderson, & R. J. Krajewski. (1980). *Clinical supervision: Special methods for the supervision of teachers.* New York: Holt, Rinehart and Winston.

Gordon, S. (1991). *How to help beginning teachers succeed.* Alexandria, VA: Association for Supervision and Curriculum Development.

Keefe, J. W., & J. M. Jenkins. (1997). *Instruction and the learning environment.* Larchmont, NY: Eye on Education.

Killion, J., & C. Harrison (2005). Roles of school based coach. *Teachers teaching teachers,* 1(3). Oxford, OH: National Staff Development Council.

Lyons, Carol A., & Gay Su Pinnell. (2001). *Systems for change in literacy education.* Portsmouth, NH: Heinemann.

Rowley, J. (1999). The good mentor. *Educational Leadership,* 56(8), 20–22.

Shaw-Baker, M. (1995). *Making the difference for teachers.* Thousand Oaks, CA: Corwin.

Snyder, K. J., & R. H. Anderson. (1988). *Managing productive schools.* Orlando, FL: Academic Press.

Thompson, D. P. (1996). *Motivating others; Creating the conditions.* Larchmont, NY: Eye on Education.

COACHING BOOSTERS

Glickman, C. et al. (2004). Observing skills. In *Supervision and instructional leadership.* Boston, MA: Allyn & Bacon, pp. 256–284.

Greene, T. (2004). *Literature review for school-based staff developers and coaches.* Oxford, OH: National Staff Development Council. Retrieved June 4, 2006 from http://www.nsdc.org/library/schoolbasedlitreview.pdf

Sullivan, S., & J. Glanz. (2000). *Supervision that improves teaching: Strategies and techniques.* Thousand Oaks, CA: Corwin Press, Inc.

COMPETENCY 5

MODELING AND COACHING EFFECTIVE TEACHING STANDARDS

COMPETENCY STATEMENT

Develop the skills to help interns and entry-level teachers translate content knowledge and pedagogy into successful classroom instructional behaviors.

KNOWLEDGE BASE HIGHLIGHTS

♦ *Brimijoin, Marquissee, & Tomlinson, 2003:* "Informal and formal data about student learning not only shape instruction but also determine its effectiveness."

♦ *Danielson, 1996:* Instructional decisions are purposeful. "Activities and assignments are not chosen merely because they are fun. They are selected or designed because they serve the instructional goals of the teacher as guided by students' interests and strengths."

♦ *Joyce and Showers, 1980:* "The importance of feedback and coaching for individuals who are expected to acquire skills is a critical component in the process of learning. Without coaching, the skill attainment level may be as low as 15 percent; whereas with coaching, there is a 90 percent level of direct transfer in the area of skill acquisition."

♦ *Kauchak and Eggen, 1998:* "Learning to teach involves not only the understanding of content and how to translate that subject matter into an understandable form, but also knowledge about the process of teaching and learning themselves. Knowledge of teaching and learning is the information we gather from research and the experiences of expert teachers that help us understand the connections between teaching and learning."

♦ *Moore, 1998:* "Teachers play many roles some of which interlock and overlap….The first and most notable role performed by a teacher is that of instructional expert: the person who plans, guides, and evaluates learning."

♦ *Wiggins & McTighe, 2005:* "As in all design professions, standards inform and shape our practice….These standards provide a useful framework to help us identify teaching and learning priorities and guide our design of curriculum and assessments."

MENTORING COMPONENTS

According to Danielson (1996), "the complexity of teaching can be daunting for those new to the profession. Teaching is one of the few professions in which novices must assume the same responsibilities as veterans in the field" (p. 55). How often has a first-year teacher been assigned the classes no one wanted to teach, or given the teaching load requiring multiple lesson preparations, or the room located in the gym or an isolated trailer? How often have we sent the message, "I paid my dues; now it's your turn. Sink or swim!" (Pattersen, 2005).

Why must we rethink our practice to better prepare interns and first-year teachers for the teaching environments within schools? We know the teaching profession is complex; we can't make it easy. But we can make the transitions easier and more rewarding. The challenge, then, is for the mentor teacher to help the novice organize the teaching tasks in order to master the complex details that are needed to become more skillful. By understanding both national and local standards, modeling and sharing effective instructional practice, sequencing the tasks and allowing practice, providing descriptive feedback, and coaching performance, you can offset the stress and isolation most novices experience.

Exhibit 5.1 is an overview of the components to successful coaching and mentoring of interns presented by Jones and Jambor (1996) in their guide for developing an intensive teacher-mentoring program in their school system.

UPDATING WHAT WE KNOW ABOUT TEACHING AND LEARNING

We are experiencing shifting views on perspectives of teaching and the ways researchers view learners and learning. An effective mentor may need to brush up on what's current in the field as it relates to instructional expertise. Exhibit 5.2 is a quick overview to help you identify recent trends in authentic pedagogy.

EXHIBIT 5.1. COMPONENTS FOR TEACHER INDUCTION AND MENTORING

Component	What it Does	How to do it	Value	Comments
Theory	Provides rationale and description of the skill or technique including potential uses.	Readings, lectures, films, discussions, etc.	Raises awareness. Increases conceptual control of a subject.	When used alone, theory rarely results in skill acquisition or transfer to classroom.
Modeling or Demonstration	Enacts the teaching strategy or skill.	Live interactions with students.	Has considerable effect on awareness; some effect on knowledge. Increases mastery.	Modeling alone is unlikely to result in transfer to the classroom.
Practice	Gives experience with the new skills in a nonthreatening setting.	Simulation of the event with both large and small groups of students.	Practice is a good way of acquiring the skill or strategy.	Practice is an effective way to develop competence in a variety of settings.
Feedback	Offers a system for reflecting on level of learning and implementation.	Can be self-administered or provided by peers or coaches.	Results in a greater awareness of one's teaching performance.	Feedback changes behaviors over the long term.
Coaching	Builds rapport, support, and technical assistance and increases total commitment of everyone involved.	Uses consultants: peers, supervisors, trainers, and professors.	Helps teachers to self-analyze and continually make appropriate adjustments in their performance.	This aspect is necessary for the internalization of the new learning.

Adapted from a staff development leadership teams training (1984) Columbus, Ohio, Ohio Department of Education. Taken from Joyce, B., and B. Showers (1980, February). Improving inservice training, the message of research. *Educational Leadership*, 37, 279–385, in Jefferson County Board of Education, *Reforming education: One classroom at a time*. Birmingham, AL. Reprinted with permission.

EXHIBIT 5.2. CONTEMPORARY VIEWS OF TEACHING AND LEARNING

Principle	Key Concepts
1. Nature of the Learning Process	Learning is active; it a process of discovering and constructing meaning from information and experiences filtered through the learner's perceptions.
2. Goals of the Learning Process	Ultimately, the learner needs to create meaningful, coherent representations of knowledge and skills.
3. Construction of Knowledge	Learners need to construct their own understanding of knowledge rather than having it delivered or transmitted to them.
4. Higher-Order Thinking	Higher-order thinking strategies help the learner develop creative and critical thinking skills. Learners need to think about their own learning tactics.
5. Motivational Influences	Learners are responsible for what and how much they learn and remember.
6. Intrinsic Motivation	Learners are naturally curious and enjoy learning.
7. Developmental Constraints	Learners progress through states of physical, intellectual, emotional, and social development. These aspects must be considered in the learning process.
8. Social and Cultural Diversity	Social interactions and communication in the classroom enhance learning. Learners can and should learn from one another.
9. Individual Differences in Learning	All learners, regardless of ethnicity, race, gender, physical ability, or socioeconomic status, have different capabilities and preferences for learning styles and strategies.
10. Cognitive Filters	Personal beliefs, thoughts, and understanding resulting from prior learning and interpretations become the learner's platform for constructing new information and interpreting experiences.

Adapted from Kauchak, D., and P. Eggen. (1998). *Learning & teaching: Research-based methods.* Boston: Allyn & Bacon, p. 10. Based on the American Psychological Association's published *Learner-centered psychological principles: Guidelines for school reform* (Presidential Task Force on Psychology in Education, 1993). Reprinted with permission.

Kauchak and Eggen (1998) point out that these general principles focus us on the "centrality of our students in the learning process" (p. 11). They emphasize that there is a major shift in the role of the teacher from information giver to instructional facilitator. Essential to this role are the tasks of actively involving students to think about their learning and "finding ways to make classrooms comfortable and stimulating places to learn—places where students feel part of a community of learners." (Kauchak & Eggen, 1998, p. 11; Danielson, 1996).

Keefe and Jenkins (1997) point out that the constructivist view of learning is evident in contemporary cognitive views of effective teaching and learning. In this approach the learner is an active participant, requiring "participation and interaction with mentors, materials, and meaning. These are the three M's of active learning which directly challenge the assumptions of traditional, largely passive learning and instruction" (p. 53). In this system, teachers are facilitators and coaches who identify with the following beliefs associated with active instructional practice:

♦ Teachers know and use prior student knowledge to extend previous learning.

♦ Teachers foster problem solving and higher-order thinking over passive learning strategies.

♦ Teachers ask students to express their learning in multiple ways that interconnect the processes of many ways of knowing and performing—speaking, writing, acting, singing, dancing, interacting, interpreting, and creating.

♦ Teachers see themselves as facilitators, guides, and coaches empowering learners to be self-leaders in the learning process.

♦ Teachers and students work together to build a community of learners based on mutual respect, trust, and common goals.

PINPOINTING THE STANDARDS FOR EFFECTIVE TEACHING

There is a growing trend for educators at all levels to use frameworks to structure conversations about teaching and learning. These guides provide several advantages. First, for newcomers to the profession, these structures give a road map of the complex interactions involved in teaching, especially if no direct assistance is provided through the school system. Second, for master teachers, they crystallize many of the things you do automatically and provide guidance for continued discussion of teaching excellence based on current research. Third, for both mentors and mentees, such frameworks provide a common ground and a common language for setting goals and objectives to improve performance. Finally, for teacher-preparation programs, these frameworks clearly define the knowledge and skills the professional community expects for exemplary teachers (Wiggins & McTighe, 2005; Jonson, 2002; Schmoker & Marzano, 1999).

The Interstate New Teacher Assessment and Support Consortium (INTASC) has created standards that form one such framework. Exhibit 5.3 is an overview of them:

EXHIBIT 5.3. INTERSTATE NEW TEACHER ASSESSMENT AND SUPPORT CONSORTIUM STANDARDS

INTASC Standard	*Description*
Standard 1	Understands the central concepts, tools of inquiry, and structure of the disciplines taught; creates meaningful learning experiences.
Standard 2	Understands how children learn and develop.
Standard 3	Understands how students differ in their approaches to learning; adapts instruction for diverse learners.
Standard 4	Understands and uses variety of instructional strategies.
Standard 5	Creates a positive learning environment.
Standard 6	Fosters active inquiry, collaboration, and group interaction through effective communication techniques.
Standard 7	Plans instruction based on knowledge of content, students, curriculum, and community.
Standard 8	Understands and uses formal and informal assessment.
Standard 9	Reflects on teaching.
Standard 10	Fosters collaborative relationships within the school community.

The framework developed by Danielson (1996) for the Association of Supervision and Curriculum Development (ASCD) correlates to the INTASC standards; we present it here to help you accomplish two goals. First, we think mentors may need to reflect on their own teaching in order to recognize clearly the various components and to assess how they perform these tasks. This analysis often moves effective teachers from unconsciously skilled to consciously skilled thinking about their teaching performance. Secondly, as we cited earlier in "Competency 2: Promoting Collaborative Learning," your clarity of purpose will be unmistakable if you have a sound framework to guide your coaching and feedback to your mentee. To meet that goal we direct your attention to the four major domains of teaching responsibility presented in this framework.

- Domain 1: Planning and Preparation
- Domain 2: The Classroom Environment
- Domain 3: Instruction
- Domain 4: Professional Responsibilities

These major domains are discussed in specific competency modules of this book. Competency 5 (this chapter) addresses Domains 1 and 3, Competencies 6 and 7 focus on Domain 2, and Competency 8 centers on Domain 4.

COACHING FOR EFFECTIVE TEACHING

DOMAIN 1: PLANNING AND PREPARATION

The first and easiest place to begin is to let the novice or first-year teacher observe and then model your lead as often as possible as you plan and implement lessons and units. Skills in Domain 1, "Planning and Preparation," are demonstrated primarily through the materials that you prepare to guide your teaching and finally through the success of those plans as implemented in your classroom. The instructional indicators emphasized in this domain are:

- Demonstrating knowledge of content and pedagogy
- Demonstrating knowledge of students
- Selecting instructional goals
- Demonstrating knowledge of resources
- Designing coherent instruction
- Assessing student learning

The teacher-preparation program has presented background information on the importance of curriculum planning and the many variables that influence the design of these plans such as the teacher, learners, motivation levels, content, materials, and time constraints. Most often a sequential planning model has been drafted that drives beginners to think about and develop goals, objectives, assessment strategies, a basic lesson plan model, interdisciplinary connections, and classroom management techniques based on the lesson approach (see Appendices F and G for samples of lesson and unit planning guides). Now is the time to see the real thing in action. Competency 5.1 is a tool to help guide the discussion on curriculum planning. Use the framework developed by Danielson as a way for you to trigger self-analysis on the part of the novice and as a mechanism for you to review important aspects in developing units and lesson plans.

COMPETENCY 5.1:
REFLECTION AND FEEDBACK GUIDE
FOR CURRICULUM PLANNING

Indicators

1a. Demonstrating Knowledge of Content and Pedagogy

What are the key concepts of the lesson/unit? What knowledge or skills are needed to learn this content? What learning problems to do students this age typically have in this area? How do you plan to minimize these learning difficulties?

1b. Demonstrating Knowledge of Students

Describe the students you plan to teach. What are their learning strengths and learning styles? What are their general interests and cultural background? Describe their general behavior and willingness to cooperate. Do you have any students with special needs? How will you accommodate them?

1c. Selecting Instructional Goals

What are your learning goals/objectives for the lesson? What specifically do you expect the student to be able to know, learn, or perform? How do you know these learning objectives are appropriate for this group of students? How do these learning goals/objectives relate to the overall school curriculum and or state standards? How will these goals/objectives be assessed?

1d. Demonstrating Knowledge of Resources

What instructional materials and resources have you located to support this lesson/unit? Can you think of any other resources that would be useful? How will you use technology to enhance the lesson/unit?

1e. Designing Coherent Instruction

Describe how you will structure the lesson/unit. How will the learning activities/content be sequenced? How do you plan to keep students actively involved in the lesson/unit?

1f. Assessing Student Learning

Explain how your assessment strategies are aligned to your instructional goals. What assessment tools have you designed? How do your tests and performance assessment criteria align to your teaching objectives and standards? How are students involved in the classroom assessment process?

From Danielson, C. (1996). *Enhancing professional practice: A framework for teaching.* Alexandria, VA: Association for Supervision and Curriculum Development. Adapted and reprinted with permission.

The research on teacher planning shows that most teachers do not write objectives (because most of them are provided in teacher guides) and they do not develop detailed plans. Rather, they plan and record activities in "a shorthand, cryptic fashion" (Kauchak & Eggen, 1998, p. 93). However, effective teachers do screen these objectives, adapt the best ideas from teacher guides that work, and delete the ones that do not prove helpful. Master teachers have a wealth of past experiences to draw upon, not to mention files of materials and resources, but beginning teachers have to start building their stock of teaching aids. Planning, although time-consuming, gives the beginner the needed structure to design a lesson, ensuring that no essential parts have been overlooked. We know that as teachers become more skillful, many of these processes become embedded and the concrete reminders are no longer necessary.

To assist novices, you might jointly plan a lesson or unit together or critique a lesson the beginner has already developed. This step in the process allows the master teacher to think aloud as he or she goes through the process of developing or reviewing a particular lesson and to check for understanding. More important, this interaction gives the novice the benefit of seeing an experienced teacher move from plan to implementation, especially when such information is not written down (Roe & Ross, 1998). Exercise 5.1 is an activity to help interns and first-year teachers make use of resources that are employed during curriculum planning.

EXERCISE 5.1. CURRICULUM SCAVENGER HUNT

Identify the curriculum tools you use:

- Course syllabi
- Curriculum guides
- Teacher's edition of textbooks
- Teacher's plan book
- Teacher's grade book or computer record system
- School district policy manual
- Teacher handbook
- Student handbook
- Brochures and flyers about the school

- State standards
- Content curriculum standards
- Assessment tools—tests and performance rubrics
- Teacher professional library
- Library collection as it relates to content area
- CD-ROMs and other software related to content area or teaching tasks
- Internet-teacher lesson plan library

Can you think of anything else? List them here:

♦ _____

♦ _____

♦ _____

♦ _____

Ask your mentee to locate and review these curriculum resources and materials and respond to the following statements:

I.   I never knew that...(think about the new data and factual information you experience).

II. I never thought of that...(focus your comments on an additional way of perceiving factual information, data, or knowledge).

III. I never felt that...(connect your responses to your inner-directed way of knowing).

IV. I never appreciated that...(center your comments on a sense of recognition that your experiences can be enhanced by what others have created or done).

V.   I never realized that...(focus your responses on an awareness of overall patterns and themes that you observe or experience).

Adapted from Belenchy, M. F., B. M. Clinchy, N. R. Goldberger, and J. M. Tarule. (1986). *Women's way of knowing: The developmental self, voice, and mind.* New York: Basic Books.

An overview of these materials helps the novice see the bigger picture. The teacher-preparation program has probably emphasized thorough planning with very detailed lesson or unit plans. Master teachers often do not have extensive plans, but novices need to be able to express what and how they plan to accomplish their targeted instructional goals. For you, the mentor teacher, these detailed plans provide insight into the novice's ability to develop well-sequenced content based on the needs of students.

DOMAIN 3: INSTRUCTION

Prevention of problems is the key to success in any teaching situation. The novice needs to plan for every instructional minute and have a back-up plan when things don't go as scheduled. Planning a lesson is the first step, targeting and developing assessment tools is the second step, and implementing the lesson is the third step. Mentors might consider the following ways to help novices implement lessons.

TEACH A LESSON

You could teach a lesson and ask the novice to observe and record your behaviors by completing an observation form. For a first-year teacher, you could videotape your lesson and give it to mentee to review. Competency 5.2 is a sample form to guide their observations.

Interns and first-year teachers need structured opportunities to discuss and analyze their own teaching behaviors and the practices of skilled experts. These discussions help them to assess the effects of teaching and to develop mental models of ways to improve their instruction. Hole & McEntee (1999) tell us that "the ordinary experiences of our teaching days are the essence of our practice. Using a guide to reflect on these experiences—either individually or with colleagues—is an entry to improving our teaching" (p. 34).

CO-TEACH A LESSON

You could coteach a lesson, modeling teaching behaviors, and then ask the mentee to teach a similar lesson. Each would observe the other, take notes, and give feedback. Competency 5.3 is a guide that you could use to help reflect on performance.

COMPETENCY 5.2:
ANALYSIS OF INSTRUCTIONAL DELIVERY

Lesson Title:_____ **Level:**_____

Teacher: _____ **Date:** _____

Directions: As I teach this lesson, jot down the behaviors you observe that show evidence of how I implemented this lesson.

Transition:

♦ How do students enter the room?

♦ What procedures appear to be in place (noninstructional and instructional)?

♦ How do I establish a positive/cooperative learning climate?

Beginning the Lesson:

♦ How do I get the students' attention focused on the learning?

♦ How does the lesson relate to students' experiences?

♦ What do you think the objectives are for this lesson? How do students know the objectives?

Conducting the Lesson:

♦ Describe in detail how I sequence the lesson. Number each step.

♦ How are students actively engaged in the lesson?

♦ How do I check for understanding? How do I assess student learning?

♦ How do I accommodate different learning styles?

Ending the Lesson:

♦ How do I conclude this lesson?

♦ What follow-up activities do I assign, if any?

Back-up Plans:

♦ What supplemental materials or extension activities do I use to accommodate learning for students with individual differences?

♦ What classroom management techniques do I use to keep students on task? How do I redirect students who are off task?

Competency 5.3: Reflection and Feedback Guide for Instructional Delivery

Indicator	Growth Area	Skillful	Strength
3a. Communicating Clearly and Accurately Elements: • Directions and procedures • Oral and written expression			
3b. Using Questioning and Discussion Techniques Elements: • Quality of questions • Discussion techniques • Student participation			
3c. Engaging Students in Learning Elements: • Representation of content is appropriate for learners • Activities and assignments are cognitively engaging • Grouping of students are productive • Instructional materials and resources support the instructional goals • Structure and pacing is clear and coherent			
3d. Providing Feedback to Students Elements: • Quality: accurate, descriptive, constructive, specific • Timeliness			
3e. Demonstrating Flexibility and Responsiveness Elements: • Lesson adjustment • Response to students' questions and answers • Persistence in seeking effective responses from students showing difficulty in learning.			

From Danielson, C. (1996). *Enhancing professional practice: A Framework for teaching.* Alexandria, VA: Association for Supervision and Curriculum Development. Adapted and reprinted with permission.

Current research on training new teachers strongly supports the notion of co-teaching with novices to ease job transition. This aspect accomplishes several things. First, it builds in a guided practice aspect into the teaching experience where any misconceptions or inadequate skill can be detected early and corrected before the solo performance. Second, it permits the novice to see you teach the various parts of the lesson—beginning, middle, and end—and then to follow your teaching style or approach. Finally, it allows the novice to reflect on your teaching as it relates to the framework used and on his or her own teaching for self-analysis and correction. Mentors might consider co-teaching more often during the early part of the experience or school year and then gradually reducing the contact to meet the needs of the mentee.

SAMPLE LESSONS

You might provide copies of sample lessons and ask the novice to use them as the basis for upcoming lessons. Review what Cangelosi (1997) tells new teachers about paying particular attention to the first week's learning activities. Discuss with your mentee the design of those lessons that should be planned early in the year:

- ◆ Develop lessons for the first few weeks of school that require simple directions, are challenging but permit all students to be successful, and involve all students at the same time. This may not be the best time for group work and a great deal of student interaction and movement until the rules and class procedures have been established.

- ◆ Develop lessons that allow you to monitor student engagement and interaction. Plan lessons that provide time to observe students and collect information about their needs and interests that will be useful in planning future lessons.

- ◆ Develop lessons that help you to discourage off-task behaviors and to reinforce on-task behaviors and student performance.

ASSESSING AND MONITORING STUDENT LEARNING

The next step in planning and designing instructional learning is helping novices reflect on the extent to which the assessments and learning activities they design align to stated goals and objectives. Wiggins and McTighe (2003) suggest a framework that would help all teachers in planning instruction that centers on big ideas, essential questions, and authentic student performance. This framework consists of the following processes:

- ◆ Determine learning goals;

- ◆ Collect, analyze and summarize evidence from multiple sources of data to determine how well students are doing on external accountability tests and the extent to which they really understand what they are learning;

♦ Consider the root causes of present achievement and then implement systematic actions to address root causes, promote enduring learning, and increase test scores (p. 55).

We think working collaboratively with novices on assessing student work is a good place to begin developing their ability to learn what standards mean for teaching and learning and what assessment evidence needs to be collected. As part of instructional coaching, effective mentors work with beginning teachers and spend time on analyzing student work samples. Here is a guide to help mentors focus their mentees on instructional artifacts.

COMPETENCY 5.4:
ANALYSIS of STUDENT WORK

Teacher _____   Grade_____ Subject _____
Lesson Topic _____   Date _____

Danielson 1e, 3a, 3c, 3d

Attach activities or assignments that engaged students in learning about the topic or concepts presented in the lesson. (i.e., a worksheet, a homework or class assignment, project guidelines, a problem to solve). Code these assignments to specific objectives.

Provide several examples of student work to this assignment which reflect the full range of student abilities, gender and ethic backgrounds in the class. Include any feedback you provided to the students on their work.

4a

Write a brief commentary about the assignment addressing the following issues:

• What prior knowledge and or skills did the students need to have in the context of this assignment? 1a, 1b

• How did this assignment or activity help the students to develop their understanding of the topic or concepts presented in the lesson? What learning objectives do these assignments reflect? 1a, 1b

• What do the samples of student work tell you about their levels of understanding? How do these levels vary by ability, gender, and ethnic differences? 1f, 3c

• How will the students use your feedback? 3d

Skillful mentors invite new teachers to look deeply at students' work by showing how they know when students' work is good enough to meet school level benchmarks and standards. Mentors and mentees in a collaborative assessment conversation read and review selected student work samples that represent low level to high levels of performance across ability, gender, and ethnic differences. Then they:

♦ Describe the work without judgmental comments

♦ Ask questions about the work, the student, and the assignment

♦ Speculate about the goal and/or learning objective

♦ Listen to the teacher who gives the situational context of the work

♦ Discuss implications for teaching and learning

After analyzing and discussing student work samples, mentors ask their mentees to reflect on performance assessment standards for beginning teachers and how they are meeting them. Competency 5.5 provides a suggested format.

IMPLEMENT THE COACHING CYCLE

Once you are sure the novice can handle all parts of the lesson successfully, then it's time for the novice to take on the whole lesson, from planning to execution, under your supportive guidance. For interns, this aspect can be managed easily since they are assigned to a cooperating teacher. However, for first-year teachers, the responsibility is already assumed. The mentor teacher may need to depend on videotaping, other support teachers, and class observations to monitor in this area.

As the novice develops and practices his or her instructional behaviors, remember to provide time for follow-up conferencing and coaching after teaching episodes. Depending upon time available, this may be a quick 10-minute conversation or a formal conference. Your mentoring plan should include both types. Encourage the novice to self-assess first, and then you can expand that analysis based on your descriptive notes or comments. During the formative practice phases, you may want to avoid evaluating the performance. Interns and first-year teachers are very sensitive to any evaluative comments and tend to immediately associate them with a final course grade or performance appraisal. We suggest letting novices evaluate themselves while you provide specific examples to support or challenge their assessment.

However, there will come a time when you will need to convey exactly where the performance is falling on the continuum. If you are unsure or uncomfortable with this part of the mentoring process, don't hesitate to involve the college supervisor for assistance if you are a cooperating teacher. If you are a first-year teacher mentor, you might simulate an observation that will be given by the school administrator using the prescribed evaluation form. As the mentor, you might work with the principal in deciding when the first official visit might occur in order to coach your mentee to the best performance possible.

COMPETENCY 5.5:
REFLECTION AND FEEDBACK GUIDE
FOR ASSESSMENT PERFORMANCE
STANDARDS

INTASC Standard 8: Assessment			
Understands and uses formal and informal assessment strategies to evaluate and ensure the continuous intellectual, social, and physical development of the learner.			
MY PERFORMANCE EXPECTATIONS			
Performance Indicators	*Below*	*Meets*	*Exceeds*
8.1 Selects, constructs, and uses assessment strategies appropriate to the learning outcomes			
8.2 Uses a variety of informal and formal strategies to inform choices about student progress and to adjust instruction			
8.3 Uses assessment strategies to involve learners in self-assessment activities to help them become aware of their strengths and needs, and to encourage them to set personal goals			
8.4 Evaluates the effects of class activities on individuals and on groups through observation of classroom interaction, questioning, and analysis of student work			
8.5 Maintains useful records of student work and performance and can communicate student progress knowledgeably and responsibly			
8.6 Solicits information about students' experiences, learning behavior, needs and progress from parents, other colleagues, and students			

SUMMARY

*"There are three things to remember when teaching. Know your stuff,
know whom you are stuffing, and then stuff them elegantly."*

Lola May

We know there is no one way to teach, encourage interns and beginning teachers to follow your lead and then adapt techniques according to their emerging teaching style. The purpose of this module is to outline a systematic process for helping you to assist novices in translating content knowledge and skills into successful classroom instructional behaviors. Understanding and applying the following five components for teacher induction and mentoring should move you well along way to becoming an effective coach and mentor.

◆ Knowing contemporary views and teaching standards

◆ Modeling and demonstrating effective instructional behaviors

◆ Providing practice and reflection

◆ Coaching performance

◆ Sharing constructive feedback

Competency 5.6 is a reflection tool to help novices build on what they learn from you.

COMPETENCY 5.6:
REFLECTION AND FEEDBACK GUIDE
FOR PLANNING, ASSESSING, AND
INSTRUCTIONAL DELIVERY

	What I Know	*What I Want to Know*	*What I Learned*	*What I Might do Differently*
Planning				
Assessing Student Learning				
Instructional Delivery				

REFERENCES

Belenchy, M. F., B. M. Clinchy, N. R. Goldberger, & J. M. Tarule. (1986). *Women's way of knowing: The developmental self, voice, and mind*. New York: Basic Books.

Brimijoin, K., Marquissee, E. and C.A. Tomlinson. (2003). Using data to differentiate instruction. *Educational Leadership*, 60(5), 70–73.

Cangelosi, J. S. (1997). *Classroom management strategies: Gaining and maintaining students' cooperation*. White Plains, NY: Longman.

Danielson, C. (1996). *Enhancing professional practice: A Framework for teaching*. Alexandria, VA: Association for Supervision and Curriculum Development.

Hole, S., & G. McEntee. (1999). Reflection is at the heart of practice. *Educational Leadership*, 56(8), 34–37.

Jones, R., & M. Jambor. (1996). *Reforming education one classroom at a time: A guide for developing an intensive mentoring program.* Birmingham, AL: Jefferson County Board of Education.

Joyce, B., & B. Showers. (1980). Improving inservice training: The message of research. *Educational Leadership,* 37, 279–385.

Jonson, K. (2002). *Being an effective mentor: How to help beginning teachers succeed.* Thousand Oaks, CA: Corwin Press, Inc.

Keefe, J. W., & J. M. Jenkins. (1997). *Instruction and the learning environment.* Larchmont, NY: Eye on Education.

Kauchak, D., & P. Eggen. (1998) *Learning and teaching: Research-based methods.* Boston: Allyn & Bacon.

Moore, K. (1998). *Classroom teaching skills.* New York: McGraw-Hill.

Pattersen, M., (2005). Hazed. *Educational Leadership,* 62(8), 20–23.

Roe, B., & E. Ross. (1998). *Student teaching and field experiences handbook.* Upper Saddle River, NJ: Prentice Hall.

Schmoker, M., & R.J. Marzano. (1999). Realizing the promise of standards-based education. *Educational Leadership,* 56(6), 17–21.

Wiggins, G., & J. McTighe. (2005). *Understanding by design.* Upper Saddle River, NJ: Merrill Prentice Hall.

COACHING BOOSTERS

Bernhardt, V. (2004). *Data analysis for continuous school improvement.* Larchmont, NY: Eye on Education.

Killion, J., & C. Harrison (2005). Data coach. *Teachers teaching teachers,* 1(2). Oxford, OH: National Staff Development Council.

Oosterhof, A. (2003). *Developing and using classroom assessments.* Upper Saddle River, NJ: Merrill Prentice Hall.

COMPETENCY 6

MODELING AND COACHING EFFECTIVE CLASSROOM MANAGEMENT STANDARDS

COMPETENCY STATEMENT

Demonstrate effective classroom management principles and classroom procedures to help interns and first-year teachers establish and maintain cooperative student relationships and self-discipline.

KNOWLEDGE BASE HIGHLIGHTS

♦ *Burke, 2000:* "A cooperative classroom doesn't just happen—it evolves from many conversations and experiences."

♦ *Manning and Buche, 2007:* "All teachers must be aware of cultural and gender diversity and its impact on classroom management... No longer can educators plan classroom management procedures for the majority culture (whatever the majority culture is) and their perspectives of appropriate behaviors."

♦ *Schaps, 2003:* "Students in schools with a strong sense of community are more likely to be academically motivated; to act ethically; to develop social and emotional competencies; and to avoid a number of problem behaviors...."

129

◆ *Warner and Bryan, 1995:* "In order to be a successful teacher who enjoys the profession, you must have a positive discipline plan, not only for your sake, but for your students' as well. A learning environment free of disruptive behavior is not an easy goal to achieve. It is so difficult, in fact, that it is the number one reason why teachers leave the profession."

◆ *Wong and Wong, 1991:* "The first thing you need to know is how to manage a classroom full of students. You were not hired to teach third grade, coach football or teach English. You were hired to take a group of possibly disinterested, howling and unruly people and turn them into interested, disciplined, and productive learners in a well-managed environment."

CREATING THE COOPERATIVE CLASSROOM

Student interns and first-year teachers have learned about effective classroom management techniques, studied the various content disciplines, and perhaps even written a classroom management plan as an assignment within the teacher-preparation program. However, having a classroom management plan on paper is quite different from implementing it in front of 30 living, breathing, and glaring students. We understand the hesitancy of some mentoring teachers in regard to "turning the classroom over" to a preservice intern. Whether it is the beginning of the school year and you are getting your class into shape, or the end of the year, you can't allow control to go by the wayside; letting an inexperienced college student be responsible for the student discipline is unnerving for many cooperating teachers and administrators. However, it is just as nerve-wracking to have a first-year teacher on your team or grade level who has little control of the classroom and spends most of his or her time yelling at students in what seems to be a never-ending power struggle. Master teachers know classroom management involves more than just teaching a lesson; it involves creating the conditions for teaching students to cooperate with you and with one another. Now how do we help mentees to do likewise?

WHAT'S YOUR CLASSROOM MANAGEMENT STYLE?

The mentoring teacher can be a tremendous help to interns or first-year teachers in maintaining order and discipline in the classroom. To effectively train novices in the most productive discipline strategies, mentors must first assess their own classroom management techniques and processes. A simple reflection on each of the following questions will provide cooperating and first-year mentors with a conscious guide in outlining what you believe and what you expect in your classroom. This guide might be useful in communicating needed information to novices about successful classroom management practices.

Exercise 6.1. Classroom Management Reflection

Think about these questions. Jot down your responses so you can reflect on what you do.

Topic	Question	Belief or Practice	Reason
Rules and Procedures	What are your classroom rules? Should students give input for the rules and consequences?		
Consequences	Do all students receive the same consequences for the same misbehavior? If not, what types of students are the exception? What types of behavior can you ignore? How do you handle off-tasks behaviors?		
Rewards	Do you believe in rewarding students for good behavior? If so, what types of rewards do you use?		
Assistance	When is it appropriate and effective to inform parents of their child's misbehavior? What types of offenses should be handled by the administrative team?		

First Things First!

For the Intern

The intern will most likely be as apprehensive about managing the classroom as you are. Probably the only ones who are not apprehensive about the transition are the students. They might see this as an opportunity to take advantage of a situation (similar to a substitute teacher day) or to withdraw and not be a participant in the learning. It is your responsibility as the cooperating teacher to give the students an orientation to the new situation. Take a few minutes to inform students of your expectations. *It is crucial that the intern be present when this is done so that he/she can hear the same information you communicate to students.* Let the students know that the same school rules, class rules, and procedures will apply when the intern is teaching or managing the classroom. Be positive and confident about this transition when speaking to the students; they will pick up on any of your concerns and could sabotage the intern's efforts.

It is also important to the success of the intern to inform him or her of the school rules and classroom rules and procedures. Ideally, you have already conducted the conference concerning classroom expectations before the intern is introduced to various classes. Any type of written handouts, such as rules, procedures, or letters to parents concerning discipline, would boost the intern's confidence in modeling your discipline style. To orient the intern to your discipline style and classroom procedures, try the following:

- ◆ Provide a copy of the system, school, and classroom discipline codes.

- ◆ Make a list of classroom procedures and expectations (e.g., restroom breaks, water breaks, trips to lockers, tardiness, etc.) and discuss them with the intern.

- ◆ Inform the intern of any student who has special needs.

- ◆ Inform the intern of any student's parents who might be difficult.

- ◆ Let the intern know of any other structural or organizational information that is essential to success.

Competency 6.1 is an example of how the conference about classroom management might be handled.

COMPETENCY 6.1: CLASSROOM MANAGEMENT CONFERENCE

Beginning of Conference

♦ Thank the intern for being present and patient during the introduction in each class. This will help the intern relax and feel less intimidated.

♦ Tell the intern that later in the conference you will discuss any specific students or situations that need special attention.

♦ Ask the intern to describe any courses or field experiences that assisted with classroom management.

♦ Ask if the intern has developed a classroom management project and, if so, take a look at it. Review the plan and ask questions about it to expand critical thinking, especially in areas that are not addressed or not fully developed.

♦ Inquire how confident the intern feels about disciplining students. Ask about specific concerns.

Middle of Conference

♦ Show the intern the various discipline codes (system, school, and classroom) and explain each and give him or her a copy of the school handbook, for example.

♦ Let the intern know exactly what type of misbehaviors that you do *not* want the intern to handle (e.g., fights, weapons, drugs) and why. Also, give the intern exact procedures for informing you of serious misbehaviors.

♦ Review the classroom procedures that have been established for students, such as restroom breaks, water breaks, etc. Ask the intern if he or she is planning any activities that might need a new procedure for the classroom. If the intern shares an activity idea with you, discuss it with the intern or table it for a conference that is closer to the actual teaching time. This is also the time that you would inform the intern of any student who has special needs or requires special consideration when teaching.

♦ Inform the intern of any child's parents who could be difficult to work with if their child receives a consequence from the intern. All this information could be overwhelming for the intern. If you need to let the intern digest the discipline codes and have a second conference to discuss students in the classroom, then do so.

♦ Offer your support. Ask the intern what kind of help would be useful. Establish a communication system so intern can alert you if he or she needs help in managing a particular lesson or class.

End of Conference

♦ Provide several helpful tips you use when managing a classroom or about disciplining a student. The topic of classroom management usually has such a negative sound to it that just talking about it helps to reduce stress and anxiety.

♦ Ask the intern to summarize what you have said. Bring a little humor to the subject and reassure the intern that you will be in the classroom to assist at any time. Coach the intern to be proactive by watching and listening for potential problems. Other tips to consider during this conference phase:

  • Share your best, worst, and funniest moments when you disciplined students.

  • Describe your strengths in this area and areas that you would like to improve.

  • Share your overall thoughts on effective classroom management.

  • Stress the importance of showing confidence when working with students.

FOR THE FIRST-YEAR TEACHER

We think it's critical that mentors and mentees reflect together during preplanning days and share responses in the form of a reflection dialogue about classroom management procedures for the first weeks of school. The reflection questions outlined in Exercise 6.1 can also serve as a guide for beginning teachers to clarify their classroom management plans. Your reflection responses as the mentor to these questions will provide your first-year teacher with additional ideas about classroom management and your reasons behind them. Most school principals expect teachers to explain all rules to the students on the first day of school. It is helpful to first-year teachers to hear how experienced teachers explain and interpret these rules and then allow an opportunity for novices to clarify and ask questions before they meet with students. Competency 6.2 is an example of how these types of conversation might develop.

COMPETENCY 6.2: REFLECTION DIALOGUE CONFERENCE

Beginning the Conference

◆ To foster a collaborative relationship, sit next to the first-year teacher and maintain eye contact while speaking.

◆ Outline the purpose of the conference as a way to share thoughts, ideas, and beliefs about classroom management.

Middle of Conference

◆ Ask the first-year teacher to share his/her written classroom management plan and procedures with you. If the beginner has not developed clear plans and procedures, ask if he/she needs assistance. If the novice indicates that he/she would like to develop it independently, ask him or her to share it with you. (See Appendix H for a sample classroom management outline.) *Whatever the circumstance, it is important as the peer mentor that you provide feedback on the classroom management plan and procedures before they are implemented with the students.*

◆ Share your classroom management plan and procedures plan with the first-year teacher. Explain why they were developed this way and why they work for you. You might find Exercise 6.1 useful here to stimulate discussion.

◆ Review the system, school, classroom, and bus codes of conduct with the first-year teacher. Be certain to fully explain the guidelines and procedures as they are outlined. You might also provide the mentee with examples of how you plan to talk to the students about the codes of conduct.

End of Conference

◆ Offer some practical tips about managing a classroom for the first week of school. Keep your comments upbeat and positive.

◆ Ask the first-year teacher to highlight the key points that you have made during this conference. Stress to the first-year teacher that you are willing to assist in any way that is needed for effective classroom management to occur in the classroom. Offer the novice an invitation to visit in your classroom or combine classes during the first week.

◆ Give the beginner the following survival checklist to guide his/her implementation of classroom rules and procedures.

COMPETENCY 6.3: CLASSROOM MANAGEMENT SURVIVAL CHECKLIST

Directions

Here's a checklist to use as you prepare for the upcoming school year. Use it to monitor your classroom management skills now and then assess them after the first two weeks of school.

Rules and Procedures

_____ Did I clearly establish the class rules? Are they positively stated? Do I have too many?

_____ Did I seek student input for classroom rules?

_____ Did I post the rules in the classroom?

_____ Did I inform the parents of the classroom rules and procedures?

_____ Did I inform the administrative team of the classroom rules and procedures?

_____ Did I review the rules and procedures by the FIRST week of school? Did I check for understanding?

_____ Did I explain and model the following classroom procedures?

- Restroom breaks_____
- Water fountain breaks_____
- Late to class_____
- Pencil sharpening_____
- Locker breaks_____
- Passes to media center_____
- Passes to other areas in the school_____
- Late assignments_____
- Make-up work for absences_____
- Working in groups_____

- Responding to questions during classroom discussions_____
- Inadequate supplies or no books_____
- Collecting and distributing materials_____

Prevention Techniques

_____Did I initiate a personal positive contact with the students and/or parents prior within the first two weeks?

_____Did I praise the students for both academic and classroom behavior performance?

_____Did I treat the students fairly?

_____Did I give effective consequences at the appropriate times?

_____Did I treat each child with dignity and respect?

_____Did I remain consistent with the classroom procedures?

_____Did I engage in appropriate conversations and discussions with the students?

_____Did I demonstrate professional demeanor in relating to students during the school day and after school hours?

_____Did I plan and teach lessons that had these characteristics:

- Directions that were simple to follow_____
- Activities that were motivating and successful_____
- Subject content that was relevant and interesting to students_____

_____Did I create an environment that promoted classroom team building?

_____Did I prevent discipline problems from occurring by using low-level intervention strategies such as scanning, proximity, the look, praise for on-tasks behaviors, and other cues?

Correction Techniques

_____Did I follow through in correcting off-task behavior? Was it effective?

_____Did I notify parents/administration of potential problems?

_____Did I have a conference with students to discuss with them of off-task/disruptive behaviors and consequences?

CLASSROOM RULES AND PROCEDURES—
SEIZE THE OPPORTUNITY!

FOR THE INTERN

In most field experiences, interns are not totally responsible for the management or discipline of students in a classroom setting. Classroom rules and norms have been established by the time the intern arrives. The job for cooperating teachers is to explain, model, and provide feedback on how well the intern is implementing the rules that have been planted and firmly rooted. We recommend that the intern not invent new rules or procedures for any reason unless you have approved them. Remember, the intern will work with the students for only a short while; if the novice invokes new ways of doing things in the classroom, you could have problems later.

After the initial conference about classroom management, your intern should have a clear picture of your expectations for students. We believe that the next step is to model how you manage the classroom. Direct the intern to take notes on how you implement the classroom rules and expectations while you teach lessons for a day or two. Stress to the intern that it is possible that only a few of the strategies could be demonstrated in one class session. You might arrange for the intern to observe other team members or grade-level colleagues, in order to expose the intern to a wide range of successful classroom management techniques. After each observation, have a conference with the intern to discuss the observation of various discipline strategies. Provide the intern with the checklist in Competency 6.4 to use while observing you and other colleagues.

COMPETENCY 6.4:
CHECKLIST FOR MANAGING
THE CLASSROOM

Classroom Management Checklist

Teacher: _____   Coach:_____

Grade: K-1-2-3-4-5-6-7-8-9-10-11-12   Start Time_____ End Time_____

Key

 ◆ Effective: The teacher is alert to student behavior at all times and deals with it in a timely manner and in a calm and assertive way. Clear expectations are communicated.

 ◆ Somewhat Effective: The teacher is generally aware of the student behavior but may miss the activities of some students. Deals with the misbehavior in a calm way but does not come across assertively.

 ◆ Growth Target: The teacher does not monitor student behavior and is unaware of what students are doing. When responding to misbehavior, the teacher appears hesitant and unsure. Responses are inconsistent.

Directions: Read each indicator and answer the question by using specific examples about what the teacher says and does to manage the classroom.	**Directions:** Summarize your observations by writing comments about what the teacher did well and what you might do differently.
Communicates Clear Expectations about Behavior (What did the teacher say?)	Effective Somewhat Effective Growth Target
Distributes Materials Efficiently (What was distributed and how was it done?)	Effective Somewhat Effective Growth Target
Manages Efficient Transitions (How did the teacher move the students into activities?)	Effective Somewhat Effective Growth Target

Provides Clear Directions (Jot down the directions given.)	Effective Somewhat Effective Growth Target

Promotes on-Task Student Behavior.
   Reinforces Desired Behavior.
   (Capture the number of times the teacher
   shows this approach.)
   • Proximity praise_____
   • Individual verbal praise_____
   • Group praise_____
	Effective
	Somewhat Effective
	Growth Target

Monitors Behavior throughout the Room
   • Scans_____
   • Circulates_____
   • Monitors the behavior of students who
     are redirected_____
	Effective
	Somewhat Effective
	Growth Target

Intervenes Appropriately when Students are
   Off-task and Nondisruptive
   • Teacher look____
   • Proximity_____
   • Uses student's name in the lesson
   • Verbal reminder of expected behavior
	Effective
	Somewhat Effective
	Growth Target

Intervenes Appropriately When Students are
   Off-task and Disruptive to the Learning of
   Others
   • Moves in_____
   • Gives choice_____
   • Changes seat_____
   • Takes aside to have a conference with
     student_____
   • Applies consequence to stated class rule
     and/or procedure_____
   • Refers to the administrative team_____
	Effective
	Somewhat Effective
	Growth Target

FOR THE FIRST-YEAR TEACHER

After the first week of school, the mentor should hold a follow-up conference, asking the first-year teacher how the classroom management plan is working. It is possible that the first-year teacher will respond with a positive statement indicating to you that there are no problems. Or, he or she could admit that certain strategies are not working with a particular student or groups of students. Whatever the case, arrange a time for the first-year teacher to observe you during a lesson so that effective strategies can be modeled. The first-year teacher could use the checklist presented in Competency 6.4 while observing you. If the first year teacher indicates that there are some problems with classroom management, then arrange a time after you model the strategies to observe the teacher. This will provide the first-year teacher with very concrete examples of correctly implemented management strategies and feedback on performance.

ESTABLISHING APPROPRIATE STUDENT RELATIONSHIPS

FOR THE INTERN

Now that the task of communicating information regarding rules and procedures to the intern has been conveyed, it is time to mention the subject of appropriate teacher-student relationships. Perhaps this is another concern of yours because sometimes novices don't understand how to show concern and compassion for students in a professional way without coming across as a "friend" to them. You know what society perceives as appropriate and inappropriate teacher–student interactions and what trouble misperceptions can cause. So, how do you teach this to your intern?

According to Jones (1980), the degree of openness a teacher wants to demonstrate determines the type of teacher-student relationship. The relationship can be characterized by:

- Almost complete openness

- Openness related only to feelings and reactions about the school environment

- An exclusive focus on teaching, in which no personal reactions or feelings are shared

It is difficult to be an effective teacher and role model to children if you don't share, at the very least, some of your feelings and reactions to the school environment and to other appropriate topics. An exclusive focus on teaching without any personal interactions can promote a negative classroom environment, where students perceive the teacher does not like them as individuals, and, therefore, they have no incentive to please the teacher. On the other extreme, sharing every emotion and reacting to all topics can create a climate that is too relaxed and inappropriate for learning. It is the balance of the three attitudes that must be modeled for the intern, using a situational approach to the three characteristics. For example, you might show how and when to share personal views on "safe" topics (e.g., pets, music, hobbies), how and when to ask stimulating questions about their views (but withholding your own), and how and when to keep controversial topics out of the classroom discussion.

The intern should be advised not to touch a student in any way or engage in a one-on-one conference behind the closed door of the classroom. As the cooperating teacher, keep a watchful eye on the intern and interactions with the students during nonacademic times (e.g., lunch time, recess, class changing, and extracurricular activities). It is most likely that the intern will want to bond quickly with the students; a natural time to do so would be during the out-of-classroom activities. If at any time you feel uneasy about your observations or a student's report regarding the intern's alleged inappropriateness, then act immediately by conferring with the student, documenting the incident, and reporting it to the college supervisor. If an intern has acted inappropriately with a student, depending on the severity, the incident/behavior should be documented in detail and shared not only with the university supervisor, but with the school administrator as well. It would be up to the administrator to notify the parent if warranted. The university is always a guest in the schools and the principal/superintendent is ultimately responsible. The key is to be proactive before everyone has to be reactive.

FOR THE FIRST-YEAR TEACHER

As the peer mentor, you will not have the same opportunities to observe the first-year teacher as you would if he or she were an intern. This does limit you in helping the first-year teacher establish appropriate teacher-student relationships. The best approach for dealing with this issue is just to observe the first-year teacher's behaviors toward the students and listen for inappropriate comments. If you feel that the first-year teacher is acting too much like a friend or buddy to the students, then tell him or her immediately. We feel that in the peer mentoring relationship, you must preserve the dignity of first-year teachers and assume that they know their limitations with students. If a problem emerges in this area, then have a conference with the first-year teacher and emphasize these points:

- The teacher-student relationship is a professional relationship, not a social or friendlike relationship.

- Extracurricular activities are for the benefit of the students, not for the teacher.

- A classroom that is too relaxed or too unstructured is not an effective learning environment for students.

- Placing hands on a student is inappropriate.

Be certain to document this type of conference just in case the problem persists. Hopefully, the first-year teacher will correct any inappropriate action as a result of your frank comments. If not, you need to be prepared with documentation to report your observations to the principal of the school.

SOCIAL INSIGHT AND WITH-IT-NESS

We know from our own experiences that without a clear understanding of your students' culture, called *social insight*, the best classroom management plans and lessons will not guarantee a classroom where students are learning. It takes more. The first time that you made a remark in the classroom causing the class to laugh (at you), you knew that you had to learn more about the world in which the students lived. Social insight is the tool that you use to peer into your students' world, especially the world of an adolescent or teenager. Gordon (1998) describes it as "an understanding of what is taking place in the classroom."

Gaining social insight is so important that without it, you are more likely to have communication problems with students that could develop into classroom management dilemmas. Students who have figured out that an intern or a first-year teacher doesn't have social insight might make remarks or insults to the teacher because they know that the inappropriate statements will not be understood. Areas in which social insight are needed include the students' speech patterns (slang), music, movie, and TV preferences, popular celebrities, newsworthy stories, and styles of dress.

What is important for the mentor to communicate is that a teacher learns the social culture of the students but doesn't become immersed in it or try to become a part of it. The culture belongs to them and it is inappropriate for the novice to emulate their dress, behaviors, or speech patterns. This is critical for young interns or first-year teachers to understand as the characteristics of their own culture could overlap with the characteristics of their students' culture, thus creating an area of too much familiarity.

Developing with-it-ness is different from developing social insight. However, both are extremely essential to a novice's success. *With-it-ness* is defined as "understanding the many behaviors taking place in the classroom and reacting appropriately" (Kounin, 1993). Kounin emphasizes that teachers increase classroom on-task behaviors by showing students that they are with-it, and can quickly and accurately detect classroom events. For example, it is common for an intern or first-year teacher to react to one student's misbehavior and forget to monitor the remaining 30 or so who could become disruptive. Why this is so common? Kounin suggests that this occurs because novices haven't learned to "have eyes in the back of their heads." You can help the intern or first-year teacher develop these "eyes" by:

♦ Demonstrating how to "watch" all of the students at the same time.

♦ Using proximity control when teaching.

♦ Acting swiftly and respectfully to an off-task or misbehaving student.

♦ Dealing with the more serious off-task behavior, when two discipline problems occur concurrently.

- Demonstrating confidence when speaking to the students.

- Using assertive eye contact and professional body language.

- Communicating understanding and sensitivity to their needs as a class and as individuals.

- Moving smoothly from one learning activity to another.

SUMMARY

*What you do speaks louder than what you say. It is by your
actions that you are defined. Aim at making a difference.
Set your students up for success, not failure.*

Classroom management for many interns and first-year teachers presents high levels of dread and anxiety. Mentor teachers can help reduce these feelings by creating ongoing dialogs, sharing their classroom management plans, and modeling appropriate teacher-student relationships. The purpose of this module is to provide strategies and techniques to help novices become successful managers of the learning environment. The following guide can be used to help mentors in giving feedback to novices during this induction phase.

COMPETENCY 6.5:
REFLECTION AND FEEDBACK GUIDE FOR CLASSROOM MANAGEMENT

Indicator	Growth Area	On Target	Skillful
2a. Creating an Environment of Respect Elements: • Teacher's interactions with students are positive. • Students show respect for one another as individuals.			
2b. Establishing A Culture for Learning Elements: • Teacher conveys enthusiasm for subject and students recognize its value. • Teacher sets high expectations for work and students take pride in that work.			
2c. Managing Classroom Procedures Elements: • Tasks for group work are organized. • Transitions occur with little loss of instructional time. • Routines are established for handling materials. • Routines are established for noninstructional duties.			
2d. Managing Student Behavior Elements: • Standards of conduct are clear to all students. • Teacher monitors student behavior and uses low-level interventions to prevent or redirect off-task behavior. • Teacher responds to misbehavior appropriately.			
2e. Organizing Physical Space Elements: • The classroom is organized to achieve the learning activities. • Teacher uses physical space and resources effectively.			

From Danielson, C. (1996). *Enhancing professional practice: A framework for teaching.* Alexandria, VA: Association for Supervision and Curriculum Development. Adapted and reprinted with permission.

REFERENCES

Burke, K. (2000). *What to do with the kid who…: Developing cooperation, self-discipline, and responsibility in the classroom.* Arlington Heights, IL: Skylight Professional Development.

Charles, C. M. (1999). *Building classroom discipline.* 6th ed. New York: Addison Wesley Longman.

Danielson, C. (1996). *Enhancing professional practice: A framework for teaching.* Alexandria, VA: Association for Supervision and Curriculum Development.

Gordon, R. (1998). How novice teachers can succeed with adolescents. *Educational Leadership,* 54(7), 56–58.

Jones, V., & L. Jones. (1995). *Comprehensive classroom management.* Needham Heights, MA: Allyn & Bacon.

Kounin, J. S. (1993, November). *Classrooms: Individuals or behavior setting.* Address sponsored by the Horizons of Knowledge lecture series, Indiana State University, School of Education, Bloomington, IN.

Manning, M.L., & K.T. Bucher. (2007). *Classroom management: Models, applications, and cases.* Upper Saddle River, NJ: Pearson Education, Inc.

Orlich, D., R. Harder, R. Callahan, D. Kauchak, R. A. Pendergrass, & A. Keogh. (1991). *Teaching strategies: A guide to better instruction.* Lexington, MA: D. C. Heath.

Schaps, E. (2003). Creating a school community. *Educational Leadership,* 60(6), 31–33.

Warner, J., & C. Bryan. (1995). *The unauthorized teacher's survival guide.* Indianapolis, IN: Park Avenue.

Wong, H., & R. Wong. (1991). *The first days of school: How to be an effective teacher.* Sunnyvale, CA: Harry K. Wong.

COACHING BOOSTERS

Chittoran, M.M., & G.A. Hoenig. (2005). Mediating a better solution. *Principal Leadership,* 5(7), 11–15.

Dr. Macs Amazing Behavior Management Advice Cite. "A wild, witty and highly practical site for educators challenged by student (mis)behavior. A definite mental health destination for teachers at their wits end in managing challenging behavior. Also provides online opportunities for teachers to help other teachers with student behavior issues." Retrieved June 4, 2006 from, http://www.BehaviorAdvisor.com

Mano, S. (2005). Moving away from the authoritarian classroom. *Change,* 37(3), 50–57.

Spitalli, S.J. (2005). The don'ts of student discipline. *The Education Digest*, 70(5), 28–31.

Teaching tolerance. Founded in 1991 by the Southern Poverty Law Center, Teaching Tolerance provides educators with free educational materials that promote respect for differences and appreciation of diversity in the classroom and beyond. Retrieved June 4, 2006 from, http://www.tolerance.org/teach/about/index.jsp

COMPETENCY 7

DISPLAYING SENSITIVITY TO INDIVIDUAL DIFFERENCES AMONG LEARNERS

COMPETENCY STATEMENT

Establish a learning environment that fosters an appreciation of diversity and respect for the cultural, ethnic, socioeconomic, and gender composition of the classroom and school.

KNOWLEDGE BASE HIGHLIGHTS

♦ *Manning and Bucher, 2007:* "Classroom management models and specific behavior strategies must show an understanding of diversity and the changing composition of contemporary classrooms. For many years, educators used the same classroom management strategies for all students, with little or no regard for students' gender, learning styles and abilities, culture, and other differences."

♦ *Edwards, 1997:* "An environment must be created in which students can learn to participate in the dominant society while maintaining distinct ethnic identities if they choose."

♦ *Midobuche, 1999:* "To be effective, teachers must treat the culture, heritage, and language of all their students *con respeto*."

♦ *Parker, 1999:* "By modifying curriculum and instruction and by addressing expressions of racism, schools can help students move beyond tolerance to acceptance, understanding, and celebration of racial and cultural differences."

148

♦ *Sadker, 1999:* "Although we have come far in ensuring that girls and boys receive equal treatment and opportunity in school, we still have a long way to go."

FACING REALITY

Many of today's schools are experiencing a change in the type of student who once dominated the halls of the public schools—white students from similar socioeconomic and religious backgrounds. Veteran teachers with more than 10 years of experience have seen the shifts in school demographics that have impacted classrooms. However, along with students from different ethnic groups, students who are homeless or economically deprived and those who have different beliefs, values, and religions from what was once considered the norm are now in the public schools. Additionally, you are teaching more students who have disabilities as more students with special needs are mainstreamed into regular classes. Without a doubt, the increase in diversity among the student population is one of the greatest and most difficult challenges facing teachers.

As a mentor teacher, how do you prepare interns or first-year teachers to deal with a diverse classroom with the respect, dignity, and understanding each student deserves to receive? The answer may be simply this: model how you desire the novice to treat all students and then give the beginner any available information about a particular child's culture, economic background, religion, or race so he or she can better teach that child.

WHAT'S THE FIRST STEP?

The first step in assisting novices in developing sensitivity towards diversity issues is to have them determine if they have any biases or misperceptions about students who might be categorized as culturally, ethnically, or socially different. One way to approach this issue is for both of you to complete a self-assessment on the topic. This method provides a baseline of questions and responses to stimulate the conversation. The important goal here is to clarify values and beliefs and see how these factors impact teaching and learning. As uncomfortable as it may seem, facing your own beliefs about diversity issues will strengthen you as a mentoring teacher and consequently challenge the novice's perspective about diversity as well.

COMPETENCY 7.1:
SELF-ANALYSIS OF DIVERSITY
ISSUES AND IMPLICATIONS

Take an honest look at what you believe about the following statements. Look at the belief statement and decide if you agree or disagree. Then jot down a personal reason or rationale for your response. During the conversation with your mentee, place a mark in the "match" column to indicate areas where the two of you agree or disagree.

Belief	Y	N	*Personal Reason/ Rationale*	M
1. Asian-American students are more motivated than other minority students.				
2. African-American students have the most discipline problems.				
3. White students are prejudiced toward minority students.				
4. Students with severe disabilities should not be mainstreamed during the school day.				
5. Language minority students should receive all of their instruction in English.				
6. At-risk students are slow learners and unmotivated to improve their learning.				
7. Intellectually gifted students are self-motivated and self-disciplined.				
8. Modifications should be made for students who hold religious beliefs outside the "norm."				
9. All students, regardless of their cultural and socioeconomic background, should only speak standard English in school.				
10. Children from low socioeconomic backgrounds are future dropouts.				
11. Female students are easier to teach than male students.				
12. Hispanic students do not adapt to the school environment with ease.				
13. Slow learners do not achieve in subjects when placed in a classroom with regular education students.				

BRIDGING THE GAP

Now that you and your mentee have examined your beliefs, had a conversation about them, and possibly had some disagreements, where do you go from here? How do you bridge the gap that possibly exists on one or more issues? Conversation needs to take place so that you and your mentee can continue to have a professional relationship. Our suggestion is to discuss the similarities in the belief statements, to build upon the positives first. Share the rationales that were written for the belief statements and make note of one another's experiences. By focusing on the positives and similarities first, discussing the differences will be much easier.

When it is time to discuss the differences in beliefs, we suggest that you establish some ground rules first. These rules need to set the tone such that the participants in this discussion will not be judgmental or try to determine who is right. The ground rules may be:

♦ Each will listen without making judgments as the differences and the rationales are stated.

♦ Each will ask questions that are related to the belief or the rationale.

♦ Each will try to gain a better understanding of the other person's beliefs as a result of the sharing experience.

Once the ground rules are established, you, the mentoring teacher, might begin the conversation first. Here is a list of steps that could be used to keep the discussion professional and informational:

♦ State the first belief that differs from your mentee's opinion. Then discuss the experience that caused you to have that belief.

♦ Ask the novice about the experience that he/she expressed that is different from yours.

♦ Listen to the novice's rationale/experience without any prejudices.

♦ Ask questions about the experience to clear any confusion in your mind.

♦ State your feelings about the belief and your reasons.

♦ Discuss how you and the novice can work together despite differences in beliefs.

It is important to remember that you and your mentee might disagree over the belief statements that are written in Competency 7.1, as well as other values and beliefs about teaching and learning. Hopefully, as a result of the discussion, there will be a deeper understanding of one another's professional views and some degree of modification and insight as these beliefs are shared. Your mentee will learn a valuable lesson as a result of the process—professionals can disagree on issues or beliefs, but still respect and work together without the disagreements interfering with educating children. Perhaps even more importantly, your intern will learn new definitions of success, including who should define it and what is required to ensure it for all students (Williams, 1999, p. 111).

How well you model this behavior will be an eminent lesson for the novice during the mentoring relationship. Carl Rogers states the predicted outcome of these conversations more eloquently: "If I can listen to what he can tell me, if I can understand how it seems to him, if I can see its personal meaning for him, if I can sense the emotional flavor which it has for him, then I will be releasing potent forces of change in him" (Rogers & Freiberg, 1994).

TIPS FOR TEACHING IN A DIVERSE CLASSROOM

Now that you've had the discussion with your intern or first-year teacher about any prejudices he or she might have about the diversity among students, the next goal is to provide the mentee with tips on how to teach the students. What do you do differently in a classroom to teach a student who is physically disabled? Or to teach a student who speaks a different language? Or to teach a student who doesn't have a place to call home? As a master teacher, you know how important it is to treat every child equally but individually. Providing an effective education that will benefit all children, regardless of their individual differences, is not an easy task to fulfill each day. However, it is another valuable lesson that you can teach the novice about meeting the needs of the students.

Being sensitive to diversity issues in the classroom is more than teaching about multicultural education or discussing different cultures or religions in the classroom. It is a way of thinking, a way of acting, and a way of planning for your lessons. In essence, certain competencies should be developed as the intern or first-year teacher begins to teach in your classroom or prepares to teach in his/her own classroom down the hall.

The Nebraska Department of Education has developed seven competencies for educators "to develop as they increase their effectiveness in multicultural instruction" (Gallagher, 1998). Although the competencies are designed to focus on multiculturalism, it is our notion that these competencies can be modified to encompass all types of diversity.

EXHIBIT 7.1. DESIGNING AND DEVELOPING STAFF COMPETENCIES— NEBRASKA DEPARTMENT OF EDUCATION

1. Recognize students' personal feelings, attitudes, and perceptions as part of their cultural norms and bias.

2. Recognize the value of ethnic and cultural diversity as a basis for societal enrichment, cohesiveness, and survival.

3. Know in teachable detail about the experiences, viewpoints, and needs of various cultural groups.

4. Acquire sensitivity to the words and actions that are insulting or hurtful to various minority groups.

5. Demonstrate through instruction and classroom or school environment how people of various groups, cultures, and backgrounds can communicate effectively and work cooperatively.

6. Use knowledge and experience of multicultural issues in selection, evaluation, and revision of instructional materials that are unbiased, factual, and complete in their treatment of minority groups.

7. Conceptualize and describe the development of the United States as a multidimensional society of ethnic and cultural diversity where diversity has been an asset and prejudice has been a destructive force in economics, cooperation, and public policy.

By developing these competencies as a mentor and then modeling the competencies for your mentee, you will be preparing her/him for the realities of educational world that lies ahead. Here are several suggestions you might demonstrate or encourage your mentee to try, as he or she plans to meet the needs of diverse groups of learners.

COMPETENCY 7.2: STRATEGIES FOR DIVERSE LEARNERS

Competency	*Suggested Strategies*
1. Recognize their personal feelings, attitudes, and perceptions as part of their norms and bias.	1. Get to know each student as a person and not as a person who is different. Talk to the students about their feelings and perceptions of others. Gather data through student interest inventories.
2. Recognize the value of diversity as a basis for societal enrichment, cohesiveness, and survival.	2. Show that you accept the value of individual differences in the classroom by involving diverse learners in activities, assigning them leadership roles on committees, and engaging them in the classroom discussions. Engage the students in cooperative learning activities to promote social growth.
3. Know in teachable detail about experiences, viewpoints, and needs of the diverse students.	3. In class discussions and lessons, include the viewpoints, needs, and experiences of the students. Show through your words and actions that you understand and value who they are and their needs. Use reflective questioning as a means of having students assess their feelings and views about issues.
4. Acquire sensitivity to the words and actions that are insulting or hurtful to diverse students.	4. Be observant of how other students are interacting with the diverse students. Listen to comments that are said about, but not to, the diverse students. Be ready to educate the students who made the comments about their insensitivity towards others. Use your school counselor as a resource person.

Competency	*Suggested Strategies*
5. Demonstrate through instruction and classroom or school environment how people of various diversities can communicate effectively and work cooperatively.	5. Implement a peer mediation program in your school. Teach your students the basics of conflict resolution and use diversity issues as examples of situations that need to be peacefully resolved. For the academic areas, involve the students in a peer tutoring relationship either to be tutored or to tutor another student.
6. Use knowledge and experience of diversity issues in the selection, evaluation, and revision of instructional materials that are unbiased, factual, and complete in their treatment of diverse students.	6. Use a variety of materials in your lesson plans. Collaborate with other teachers to collect materials and resources on diversity issues. Be certain to teach to the various learning styles of the students. It might be helpful to assess their learning styles as early into the school year as possible.
7. Conceptualize and describe the United States as a society of ethnic, economic, religious, and physical diversity where diversity has been an asset and prejudice has been a destructive force in economics, cooperation, and public policy.	7. Invite community members to speak to your class on the value of diversity in this particular community. Also, keep the students abreast of current events that are reported in the newspaper, television, or radio, or the Internet that are examples of prejudices towards diversity. Instruct the students to keep a journal of their reactions or feelings about diversity issues that are discussed in class, viewed on television, or read in the newspaper.

Adapted from the Nebraska Department of Education, *Designing and Developing Staff Competencies.*

PROGRAMS AND APPROACHES FOR DIVERSE LEARNERS

Outlined below are several examples of current programs that may be useful to you and your mentee in developing expertise in teaching diverse learners. Here is a brief description of these approaches:

Program/Strategy/Tool	*Overview*
The Responsive Classroom. Retrieved June 6, 2006 from http://www.responsiveclassroom.org/about/research.html	Used in prekindergarten through eighth-grade classes, the Responsive Classroom aims at integrating the academic and social curriculum by: • Fostering a sense of community through whole group activities • Developing positive social interactions through active listening and inclusion • Team building through reinforcement of the skills needed to be a responsive and cooperative member of the classroom
Differentiated Instruction in Mixed Ability Classrooms: ASCD Professional Inquiry Kit. Retrieved June 6, 2006 from http://www.ascd.org	Working with students with varying ability levels can prove to be a challenge to any teacher. This program seeks to: • Find ways to make sense of information and ideas • Adjust the focus of assignments • Present multiple approaches to content, skills, process, and product • Center more on students' needs rather than on teachers' needs
Cooperative Learning, Values, and Culturally Plural Classrooms. Cooperative Learning Center at the University of Minnesota http://www.co-operation.org/	Aims at using group work in heterogeneous classes to accomplish the following: • Frequent use of cooperative learning in small groups to keep student engagement high without direct and immediate monitoring of the teacher • Development of group interdependence and leadership skills • Increase patterns of interaction among students that result in diversity being valued rather than rejected.

Program/Strategy/Tool	Overview
MicroSociety: A Real World in Miniature. Retrieved June 6, 2006 from http://www.micosociety.org	A program built to tie together the academic program to the experiences of students and the realities of the work force, this program includes the following aspects: • Through simulation in a miniature community students learn to be producers and contributors in their world beyond the school doors • Participants learn to deal with real-life problems that have both ethical and moral implications • The entire school community—students, teachers, administrators, parents, and community members—interact to improve the quality of life within the school
Resiliency in Schools: Making it Happen for Students and Educators (Henderson & Milstein, 2002)	In this updated edition the authors offer scores of new resources for resilience education as well as an action plan you can use right now to build inner strength and flexibility in your students and staff. You'll learn: • What resiliency is and why it is so important • Schoolwide strategies to move students from "at risk" to resilient • How to adopt resiliency as the fourth "r" of your educational goals • Why resilient students need resilient educators • Skills and tools for resiliency building

SUMMARY

"The best things and best people rise out of their separateness;
I'm against a homogenized society because I want the cream to rise."

Robert Frost
(V. Caruana, 1998)

Schools are experiencing ever-increasing changes in the types of students that once dominated the halls and the classrooms. Today's classrooms are much more diverse than ever before, and the differences are not just limited to ethnicity. Teachers must be sensitive to the needs of all students by treating them with respect, understanding, and compassion. Even more important, educators must continually seek ways to strengthen relationships between staff and culturally diverse students in order to improve learning. Scherer (1999) reminds us that "we must know history and share it with our students. Enlarge the curriculum to include diverse voices, and go beyond tolerance to respect" (p. 7).

Interns and first-year teachers need to be able to model appropriate ways to teach diverse students and, perhaps even more important, ways to connect these students to caring adults and their peers. By being sensitive to students' needs and meeting their needs as unique individuals within the classroom, these students are given the best opportunity or environment in which to learn. As teacher mentors, we must take a strong position in urging mentees not only to be knowledgeable about issues of diversity, but also proactive in using these concepts into their teaching. "How else will minority and majority children see their own self-worth and relatedness of their lives?" (Midobuche, 1999, p. 82).

REFERENCES

Gallagher, J. (1998). Multiculturalism at a crossroads. *Middle Ground*, 1(3), 11–14.

Henderson, N., & M. M. Milstein. (2002). *Resiliency in schools: Making it happen for students and educators.* Thousand Oaks, CA: Corwin.

Manning, M.L., & K.T. Bucher. (2007). *Classroom management: Models, applications, and cases.* Upper Saddle River, NJ: Pearson Education, Inc.

Midobuche, E. (1999). Respect in the classroom: Reflections of a Mexican-American educator, *Educational Leadership*, 56(7), 80–82.

Parker, S. (1999). Reducing the effects of racism in schools. *Educational Leadership*, 56(7), 14–18.

Richmond, G. (1997). *The microsociety school: A real world miniature.* Philadelphia, PA: MicroSociety.

Rogers, C., & H. J. Freiberg. (1994). *Freedom to learn.* New York: Merrill.

Sadker, D. (1999). Gender equity: Still knocking at the classroom door. *Educational Leadership*, 56(7), 22–26.

Williams, B. (1999). Diversity and education for the 21st century. In D. Marsh (ed.), *ASCD yearbook: Preparing our schools for the 21st century.* Alexandria, VA: Association for Supervision and Curriculum Development.

COACHING BOOSTERS

Boreen, J., & D. Niday. (2003). Mentoring the teacher teaching at-risk students. In *Mentoring across boundaries: Helping beginning teachers succeed in challenging situations*. Portland, MA: Stenhouse Publishers, pp.121–134.

Elias, M., J. Zins, R. Weissberg, K. Frey, M. Greenberg, N. Haynes, R. Kessler, M. Scwhab-Stone, & T. Shriver. (1997). *Promoting social and emotional learning*. Alexandria, VA: Association for Supervision and Curriculum Development.

Holloway, J. (2003). What promotes racial and ethnic tolerance? *Educational Leadership*, 60(6), 85–86.

Marsh, D. (ed.). (1999). *ASCD yearbook: Preparing our schools for the 21st century*. Alexandria, VA: Association for Supervision and Curriculum Development.

Nieto, S. (2000). *Affirming diversity: The sociopolitical content of multicultural education*. NY: Longman.

Payne, R. (1998). *A framework for understanding poverty*. Baytown, TX: RFT Publishing.

Spencer, M.B. (2000). Ethnocentrism. In A. Kazdin (ed.), *Encyclopedia of psychology*. Washington, DC: American Psychological Association.

Thomas, R.M. (2000). *Human development theories: Windows on culture*. Thousand Oaks, CA: Sage.

COMPETENCY 8

WILLINGNESS TO ASSUME A REDEFINED PROFESSIONAL ROLE

COMPETENCY STATEMENT

Seek the knowledge, skills, and dispositions to promote attitudes of a life-long learner and teacher-leader both within yourself and those you coach and mentor.

KNOWLEDGE BASE HIGHLIGHTS

♦ *Barth, 1990:* "Teachers harbor extraordinary leadership capabilities, and their leadership is a major untapped resource for improving the nation's schools. All teachers can lead."

♦ *Buchen, 2000:* "The only leadership that will make a difference is that of teachers. They alone are positioned where all the fulcrums are for change."

♦ *Danielson, 1996:* "Educators and researchers have gradually expand-ed the definition of teaching to include not only classroom interac-tion between teachers and students but also the full range of respon-sibilities that comprise teaching."

♦ *Gabriel, 2005:* "With the growing emphasis on high-stakes testing and the advent of No Child Left Behind, many school leaders are seeking more effective organizational behavior by drawing on the leadership potential of all stakeholders, especially teachers."

♦ *Waitley, 1995:* "In the past, change in business and social life was in-cremental, and a set of personal strategies for achieving excellence was not required. Today, in the knowledge-based world, where change is the rule, a set of personal strategies is essential to success, even survival. Never again will you be able to go to your place of business on autopilot, comfortable and secure that the organization will provide for and look after you. You must look into the mirror when you ask who is responsible for your success or failure."

THIS IS A NEW DAY

Are you willing to consider a new dimension to your professional role of teacher? Dennis Waitley, author of numerous publications about high-level achievement in business, sports, and personal life, challenges us to look deep within ourselves to measure our capacity for self-leadership and change by asking ourselves these questions:

- "How do you respond to sudden, unforeseen change or challenges?"

- "Are you: A. Pragmatic, set in your ways?

            B. Flexible, adaptable to alternatives?"

- "When did you complete your education?"

This competency module is a call to individual leadership within your professional role as teacher. Are you ever a team leader or always a team member? We can no longer say: "Why doesn't the school administration or the school district do something?" Rather we must say, "Here's what I am doing to solve the problem." Waitley tells us this: "For a vision to be inspiring and worth sharing, it needs to bring out the best in all of us, not pander to the worst in us. In order to gain the respect of others, we must first earn it. We must be respectable. In order to be a role model, we must first set a positive example. In order to lead others, we must lead ourselves" (Waitley, 1995).

QUESTION ONE: CHANGE AND CHALLENGES

How do you respond to sudden change and emerging challenges in your professional setting? Do you feel threatened by current technologies, shifting ways of teaching and learning, and more demands on you as an educator with less time to prepare for these new tasks? Do you find yourself longing for the "good ole days?" Change of all kinds—economic, social, cultural, technological, political, and educational—is occurring all around us and the pace shows no sign of slowing down.

As teachers, we carry the tremendous responsibility of shepherding those in our charge into the next century and beyond. Look into the mirror. What do you see? Do you see a self-leader who responds to change or reacts to it? A proactive teacher responds to change by studying the change and taking from it the key concepts and components to create new knowledge, new teaching methods, and better interrelationships within the school community in order to enhance student learning and self-leadership ability. A self-leader asks how, why, and where things are changing so he or she can exploit the possibilities (Waitley, 1995).

According to Roland Barth (1990) in his book, *Improving Schools from Within*, a teacher-leader in the educational setting believes in the vision of building a community of learners and leaders. He outlines several reasons why opportunities for teachers to engage in school leadership may be essential. First, they offer possibilities for improving teaching conditions. Teachers often see things going on their school that bother them. Barth contends principals can view criticism from a disgruntled teacher as either a challenge to their leadership or an opportunity to empower this teacher to take action. Second, shared decision making with teachers replaces the solitary authority of the principal with a collective authority. School leadership teams provide a constructive format in which teachers can interact, consequently overcoming daily classroom isolation with students. Finally, developing a community of leaders helps transform schools into contexts for adults' as well as children's learning, and participation in leadership for both teachers and students builds community.

Barth goes on to say that when teachers are involved in the decision-making process everyone wins. Teachers' concerns are better understood and articulated by a fellow peer and important schoolwide issues receive focused attention when the adult responsible has ownership in resolving the problem. One or two administrators can no longer manage schools. "If the principal tries to do all of it, much of it will be left undone by anyone" (p. 128). In today's workplace, all stakeholders must be self-leaders involved in moving their organizations forward (Gabriel, 2005; Crowther et al, 2002).

QUESTION TWO: ADAPTABILITY AND FLEXIBILITY

Schools of the past, like most organizations, operated on a chain of command, a top-down system of decision making with a central line authority. That system is no longer operational. The new school culture must meet ever-increasing student, teacher, parent, and community demands. The global community at large expects today's schools to produce students who can achieve academically and perform competently in the workplace and teachers who can instruct at high levels of performance. The bottom line is this: What worked yesterday is not working today. WHY?

- ◆ Yesterday, the top-down chain of command was the model. Today collaboration is the norm.

- ◆ Yesterday, principals and teachers commanded and controlled. Today they empower and coach.

- ◆ Yesterday, teachers were knowledge disseminators. Today they are facilitators of learning.

- ◆ Yesterday, principals and teachers demanded respect. Today they foster self-respect, self-discipline, and self-leadership.

- ◆ Yesterday, the organization came first. Today consumers come first.

- Yesterday, teachers took orders. Today teams of teachers make decisions for school improvement.

- Yesterday, seniority and tenure signified status. Today creativity and problem solving to meet change impact job success.

- Yesterday, performance competency was assumed. Today performance competency is demanded.

Waitley (1995) informs us that self-leaders have the "ability to adapt, to assume responsibility, to have a shared vision, to empower others, to negotiate successful results, and to assume control of their behavior and life" (p. 11). How adaptable are you to the flux of change that surrounds you?

QUESTION THREE: KNOWLEDGE IS POWER

So when did you complete your education? If we are truly facilitators of learning, and if knowledge is truly power, we must be promoters of lifelong learning. Yet, how often have we frowned at the thought of going back to school for an advanced degree, or fretted at having to attend a staff development workshop, or resented being asked to mentor a colleague? Are you among the vast numbers of educated adults who don't believe they need to learn about new subjects or study those they know in greater depth?

How many of our colleagues believe that information found in books, computer programs, and training sessions has no value for them? How many still avoid the new tools of technology and refuse to utilize them in their classrooms or homes? In the blink of an eye, our world has leaped from the Stone Age to the Space Age—an age in which knowledge and information are fluid, dynamic, and flexible. An age where knowledge and information connect across disciplines and continents in seconds, and become the key to opportunity and advancement. The knowledge base is expanding exponentially, which means your formal education has a very short lifespan.

Are we creating generations of new minds who would rather sit and watch than participate and do? How often have we blamed the decline in student achievement on the television, video games, and the Internet? Yet, how many of us prefer to do just enough to get by in our career or just enough to get through the day? What exactly have we communicated to our students? Have we said, "Do as I say, not as I do?" Waitey (1995) reminds us that "knowledge starts with keeping an open mind and with the hard work of self-improvement" (p. 11). Everything we learn teaches us how to think in different ways and to connect that information to past knowledge, reshaping it and reusing it within continuously evolving mental frameworks.

And herein may lie the dilemma. Once we become experienced or we graduate from an advanced degree program, do we lose our sense of wonder? "Instead of being driven by curiosity, do we become driven to defend what we've previously researched, invented, created, marketed, or published?" (Waitley, 1995, p. 15). Linda Darling-

Hammond (1998) states that "new teacher education programs envision the professional teacher as one who learns from teaching rather than as one who has finished learning how to teach" (p. 7). This clearly sets the goal toward a career as a lifelong learner.

Today's schools are under the gun to educate a very diverse student body to higher academic standards than ever before within an increasingly complex and rapidly changing, technology-based world community. Schools must be organized to support teachers' continuous learning and mentoring. The best reason for "avoiding thinking like an expert while continuing to acquire expertise" is that your assumptions may hinder your ability to generate and work with new ideas (Waitley, 1995, p. 15).

STANDARDS FOR PROFESSIONALISM

THE RESEARCH BASE

Current trends have expanded the definition of teaching to include not only classroom responsibilities but also a range of other responsibilities that continue beyond the classroom door. As teaching becomes more grounded in research, the notion of teaching as a true profession with all its implications will become more evident (Danielson, 1996). Currently, teacher professionalism is a new field of study and much of the available research is theoretical rather than based on empirical data.

The National Board for Professional Teaching Standards (NBPTS) identifies itself as an organization committed to professional standards for teaching. The term *professional* in our society represents occupations characterized by certain attributes. Principal among these is a body of specialized, expert knowledge, together with a code of ethics that emphasizes service to clients. "The knowledge base typically provides substantial, but not complete, guidance for professional practice. Professionals possess expert knowledge, but often confront unique, problematic situations that do not lend themselves to formulaic solutions. Professionals must cultivate the ability to cope with the unexpected and act wisely in the face of uncertainly" (NBPTS, 1997).

Here are the five principles and their definitions cited by NBPTS as the foundation for the assessment of accomplished teachers. They are presented directly as written from the NBPTS Web page, http://www.nbpts.org/nbpts/standards.

♦ *Teachers are committed to students and their learning.* National Board-certified teachers are dedicated to making knowledge accessible to all students. They act on the belief that all students can learn. They treat students equitably, recognizing the individual differences that distinguish their students one from the other and taking account of these differences in their practice.

♦ *Teachers know the subjects they teach and how to teach those subjects to students.* National Board-certified teachers have a rich understanding of the subject they teach and appreciate how knowledge in their subjects is created, organized, and linked to other disciplines and applied to real-world settings. While faithfully representing the collective wisdom of our culture and upholding the value of disciplinary knowledge, they also develop the critical and analytical capacities of their students.

♦ *Teachers are responsible for managing and monitoring student learning.* National Board-certified teachers create, maintain, and alter instructional settings to capture and sustain the interest of their students and to make the most effective use of time. They are also adept at engaging students and adults to assist their teaching and at enlisting their colleagues' knowledge and expertise to complement their own.

♦ *Teachers think systematically about their practice and learn from their experience.* National Board-certified teachers are models of educated persons, exemplifying the virtues they seek to inspire in students—curiosity, tolerance, honesty, fairness, respect for diversity, and appreciation of cultural differences—and the capacities that are prerequisite for intellectual growth—the ability to reason and take multiple perspectives, to be creative and take risks, and to adopt an experimental and problem-solving orientation.

♦ *Teachers are members of learning communities.* National Board-certified teachers contribute to the effectiveness of the school by working collaboratively with other professionals on instructional policy, curriculum, and staff development. They can evaluate school progress and the allocation of school resources in light of their understanding of state and local educational objectives. They are knowledgeable about specialized school and community resources that can be engaged for their students' benefit and are skilled at employing such resources as needed. Accomplished teachers find ways to work collaboratively and creatively with parents, engaging them productively in the work of the school. (NBPTS, 1997)

PINPOINTING THE STANDARDS FOR PROFESSIONAL RESPONSIBILITIES

MODELING AND DEMONSTRATION

Your role as coach and mentor involves helping interns to understand the myriad duties and responsibilities that you do beyond teaching and managing your classes. Your attitude about these additional tasks will affect the perspective of your mentee. Most teacher-preparation programs have built in the role of teacher-leader in their programs to alert aspiring teachers that today's schools expect them to be involved in making contributions to the school and district. For example, one university's teacher-education program describes its program's philosophy as shown in Exhibit 8.1.

EXHIBIT 8.1. PROFESSIONAL EDUCATION
MODEL FOR TEACHER EDUCATION

Program Philosophy: A Metacognitive Perspective

North Georgia College & State University prepares teachers for tomorrow's classrooms—teachers who can deliver knowledge and skills in an effective manner, make informed decisions and choices, and assume leadership—first in the classroom and then within the professional community. The process which integrates these roles of *Facilitator, Decision-Maker*, and *Leader* is a metacognitive one, in that teachers must be conscious of their thinking and problem-solving processes in order to integrate and monitor the interaction of these roles. Metacognition is that ability which enables teachers to plan a course of action prior to beginning a task, to monitor themselves while executing a plan, to alter or adjust a plan consciously, and finally to evaluate the results after action has been taken.

Traditionally, the role of the teacher has included the facilitation of learning. The facilitator (teacher) is responsible for structuring the learning environment in such a way as to enable effective and efficient learning to occur. As a *Facilitator* in the teacher education program you will increase your competencies in these four areas: Subject Matter Knowledge, Individual Differences of Students, Communications including technology, and Classroom Management.

In addition, the teacher must have a knowledge base related to curriculum, methods, trends, issues, and assessment as well as a repertoire of workable principles by which appropriate curricular and classroom management decisions can be made. As a *Decision-Maker* in the teacher-education program you will increase your competence in these four areas: Assessment, Planning, Problem Solving, and Instructional Methods, Materials, and Resources.

Finally, in an educational setting where opportunities for "teacher empowerment" are increasing, the teacher must be prepared to assume a variety of leadership roles during his or her career. This concept of leadership is multifaceted and part of the mission statement for the University, in that North Georgia graduates are expected to be prepared to undertake leadership roles in their profession and within their community. As a *Leader* you will increase your competence in these four areas: Ethical Perspectives, Metacognition, Professional Leadership, and Research and Evaluation.

Examining the framework designed by Danielson (1996), we can see evidence of this trend to include the professional contributions of teachers within their school communities. Skills in Domain 4, "Professional Responsibilities," include these indicators:

♦ Reflecting on teaching

♦ Maintaining accurate records

♦ Communicating with families

♦ Contributing to the school and district

You might begin a discussion in this area by using the Competency 8.1 checklist to identify the various tasks you perform.

Once you have identified your contributions to the school, encourage interns or first-year teachers to develop records of these responsibilities as they proceed through their internship and their teaching career. Danielson (1996) tells us that teachers undertake these assignments as part of their teaching responsibility but often do not have any documentation of what they have done or the results of their work.

The big question for novices is, "How do I teach and then do all of this, too?" Your time management system, coaching suggestions, and the tools you use will form a valuable model for them to follow. Once you have identified the tasks, a timeline of when and how you manage them will be useful. If time and schedules permit, asking the intern or first-year teacher to shadow you or your colleagues as you or they participate in one or more of these tasks will provide snapshots of how teachers are involved in school improvement efforts and activities.

EXERCISE 8.1. SHADOWING EXERCISE

Directions: Ask your mentee to shadow you through a day when you have assignments both within the teaching day and beyond. Use this tool as a way to introduce your intern or first-year teacher to these professional responsibilities.

Date and Time	Event/Activity	Teacher's Role	Reflection on Event or Activity

COMPETENCY 8.1:
PROFESSIONAL RESPONSIBILITIES
CHECKLIST

Directions: List all the professional contributions you make to the school. Share these with your mentee.

School Committees	Date	Purpose	Contribution
Team Meetings	Date	Purpose	Contribution
Student Clubs	Date	Purpose	Contribution
Professional Development Activities	Date	Purpose	Contribution/ Benefits

Starting here should help the novice get the bigger picture of what teaching is all about. Now you can focus on specific areas that the intern or first-year teacher may have questions about. Competency 8.2 is a feedback tool to help you guide your mentee in Domain 4. Ask your mentee what areas concern him or her the most. Then develop a plan in which you find ways to model or demonstrate the targeted indicator.

COACHING AND FEEDBACK

Central to most teacher-preparation programs is the idea that interns and beginning teachers need to develop their skills of accurate reflection on their performance. You will find that most novices tend to do this on a superficial basis. If you feel comfortable with self-assessment, you might ask the intern to reflect with you as you evaluate your successes and possible growth areas in a lesson you teach. Let the mentee reflect individually. Then, in one of your weekly meetings, ask the mentee to share the information as suggested in Competency 8.3.

COMPETENCY 8.2: REFLECTION GUIDE

♦ Key Events

Ask your mentee to keep a journal. Entries don't have to be long, but encourage your mentee to collect stories about events occurring in the classroom.

♦ Incident Summary

Ask your mentee to review the entries for the week and select an event that interests him or her or that had a significant impact on the lesson. Ask the mentee to describe the incident objectively, answering such questions as: What events led up to this event? Why did it happen? How did I respond?

♦ Critical Reflection

Ask the mentee to explore the event, thinking about what it means to him or her and what was learned.

♦ Future Directions

Based on this analysis, ask the mentee to share how this event provided insight and new understanding about teaching and learning. What will the mentee do as a result of this individual reflection?

COMPETENCY 8.3:
REFLECTION AND FEEDBACK GUIDE
FOR PROFESSIONAL RESPONSIBILITIES

Indicator	*Growth Area*	*On Target*	*Skillful*
4a. Reflecting on Teaching Elements • Accuracy in self-assessing performance • Use in future teaching or performance			
4b. Maintaining Accurate Records Elements • Student completion of assignments • Student progress in learning • Noninstructional record keeping			
4c. Communicating with Families Elements • Information about the instructional program • Information about individual students • Engagement of families in the instructional program			
4d. Contributing to the School and District Elements • Relationships with colleagues • Service to the school • Participation in school and district projects			
4e. Growing and Developing Professionally Elements • Enhancement of content knowledge and skill • Service to the profession, such as mentoring new teachers, publishing, and presentations at conferences			
4f. Showing Professionalism Elements • Service to students seeking resources • Advocacy to ensure all students are served • Decision making within a leadership role to ensure that such decisions are based on high ethical standards.			

From Danielson, C. (1996). *Enhancing professional practice: A framework for teaching.* Alexandria, VA: Association for Supervision and Curriculum Development. Adapted and reprinted with permission.

Most internships require interns to keep a reflection log. If the intern feels comfortable with sharing this log with you, it might provide additional insight into his or her thinking processes. (See Appendix page 197 for a sample reflection guide). Continuing the reflection process into the first year of teaching may help beginners further their problem-solving skills and provide a communication mechanism to stimulate dialog within the mentorship experience.

An important part of teaching includes the assessment and monitoring of student progress. Share with your mentee your process in maintaining accurate records from such things as your grade books, computer management systems, skills checklists, project assignments, results of standardized tests, and records of noninstructional items such as absence notes, permission slips, and lunch counts. In particular, allow them to enter these records whenever feasible and become familiar with the technology you use.

Once those data have been gathered, communication of the information to school personnel and parents is essential. Acquaint your novice with your school reports to parents—PTA meetings, newsletters, open houses, report cards, conference days, and telephone contacts—and what you may do to supplement these systems with additional information. If possible, permit the novice to sit in on parent conferences and reflect on the effectiveness of the communication between you, the teacher, and the parent.

SUMMARY

Real leaders are ordinary people with extraordinary determination.

NASSP Great Quotations, 1985

We started this module with a call for self-leadership. Danielson (1996) also concludes with a parallel plea for continuing professional development, asserting that this process is the "mark of a true professional, an ongoing effort that is never completed" (p. 115). Teachers who are dedicated to seeking and remaining at the top of their profession invest much time and energy in renewing their content expertise and expanding their teaching behaviors. Many are seeking National Board certification to demonstrate their professionalism and competence, while others show service to the profession through such activities as mentoring new teachers, publishing, and presentations at conferences.

Novices need to know that the complexity of teaching includes a vast array of instructional and professional responsibilities and the reasons why they have come about in our profession. Past induction methods have left beginners to flounder on their own without any systematic assistance or encouragement as they have attempted to master these responsibilities. Teacher mentoring may be more than a sensible approach to help keep talented young teachers in the profession. It may be critical in "the light of statistics that continues to tell us that 30 percent of newcomers will quit within their first five years in the classroom" (Scherer, 1999).

Rowley (1999) affirms that quality teacher-mentoring programs need competent mentors who have positive outlooks and high levels of hope and optimism for the future of the teaching profession. The good mentor helps the new teacher "discover the same joys and satisfactions that they have found in their own career" (p. 22).

What will they see through your eyes and hear through your words?

REFERENCES

Barth, R. (1990). *Improving schools from within*. San Francisco: Jossey-Bass.

Buchen, I.H. (2000, May 31). The myth of school leadership. *Education Week*, 19(38), 1–3.

Crowther, F., Kaagan, S., Ferguson, M. & L. Hann. (2002). *Developing teacher leaders*. Thousand Oaks, CA: Corwin Press, Inc.

Danielson, C. (1996). *Enhancing professional practice: A framework for teaching*. Alexandria, VA: Association for Supervision and Curriculum Development.

Darling-Hammond, L. (1998). Teacher learning that supports student learning. *Educational Leadership*, 55(5), 6–11.

Gabriel, J.G. (2005). *How to thrive as a teacher leader*. Alexandria, VA: Association for Supervision and Curriculum Development.

——— National Board for Professional Teacher Standards (NBPTS) (1997). http://www.nbpts.org/nbpts/standards.

Rowley, J. (1999). The good mentor. *Educational Leadership*, 56(8), 20–22.

Scherer, M. (1999). Perspectives: Knowing how and knowing why. *Educational Leadership*, 56(8), 7.

Waitley, D. (1995). *Empires of the mind*. New York: William Morrow.

COACHING BOOSTERS

Center for Teacher Leadership. http://www.ctl.vcu.edu/

Resources for Teacher Leadership. http://cse.edc.org/products/teacherleadership/mentoring.asp#11

QUOTATIONS (COMPETENCIES 1 TO 8)

Caruana, V. (1998). *Apples and chalkdust. Inspirational stories and encouragement for teachers*. Tulsa, OK: Honor Books.

——— (1985). *Commitment to excellence*. Restin, VA: NASSP Great Quotations, Inc.

Estrem, V. L. (1995). *Celebrate treasures of friendship*. Edina, MN: Lighten Up Enterprises.

APPENDIX A
INTERNSHIP EVALUATION FORM

North Georgia College and State University School of Education
Internship Evaluation of Teaching Competencies

Instructions: Beside each descriptor, write the number that typifies the usual or most consistently observed performance of the Intern. The ratings should be based upon the documentation collected during the term. Use the following numerical classification:

1. Unacceptable performance [implies unsatisfactory, inappropriate, insufficient performance]

2. Minimal performance [implies below average, superficial, inconsistent performance]

3. Adequate performance [implies reasonable sufficiency for the purpose, average performance]

4. Proficient performance [implies competency above the average]

5. Skilled performance [implies adeptness, aptitude as well as proficiency]

Competencies that relate to specific internship requirements *are in italics* and are weighted more heavily in the determination of the final grades. Each of the three Sections is to be evaluated with a letter grade. At the end of this evaluation form is space to comment on the intern's strengths and professional development goals.

I. COMPETENCY AS A FACILITATOR

Indicators: Subject Matter, Individual Differences, Communication, Classroom Management:

Section I Evaluation: ☐

Subject Matter Indicators:
1. *Communicates accurate, current content clearly and sequentially.*
2. Achieves objectives through focused activities and instruction.
3. *Implements successfully a variety of appropriate strategies, approaches to materials, and learning activities.*
4. Illuminates/elaborates key concepts and monitors students' understanding through effective questioning techniques.
5. Provides opportunities for students to practice/process content.
5. Connects content to students' life experiences.
6. *Uses appropriate technology to enhance instruction of content.*
   Summary Rating:____

Individual Differences Indicators:

1. Utilizes background data to assign students to groups, materials, and/or activities.
2. Creates a positive environment respectful of ethnic, cultural, and/or special needs and learning styles.
3. Uses teaching strategies promoting cultural/ethnic, academic, gender, and disability inclusiveness.
4. Demonstrates flexibility in adapting instruction required by student performances, special needs, and/or changing conditions.

    Summary Rating:____

Communication/Interpersonal Indicators:

1. Demonstrates acceptable professional oral expression.
2. Demonstrates acceptable professional written expression.
3. Exhibits poise, self-confidence, and self-control when teaching.
4. Demonstrates tact and sound judgment in professional settings.
5. Shows appropriate enthusiasm/humor when teaching.
6. Responds positively to student questions and input in the lesson.
7. Provides general and specific reinforcement and feedback about students' academic efforts.
8. Communicates content effectively through clear directions, procedures, and explanations.

    Summary Rating:____

Classroom Management Indicators:

1. Organizes time, space, materials, and equipment for instruction.
2. Handles classroom routines efficiently and in a timely manner.
3. Secures and maintains students' attention.
4. Seeks active involvement of students throughout learning activities.
5. *Implements a management plan suitable to the developmental needs of students and the classroom context.*
6. Manages individual learning activities and a variety of group learning situations.
7. Articulates clear expectations and appropriate feedback about behavior when necessary.
8. Monitors students' behavior and on-task performance throughout the lesson.
9. Promotes on-task behavior by use of nonverbal techniques (i.e., scanning, circulating, eye contact, and proximity control).
10. Manages disruptive behavior effectively.
11. Makes transitions efficiently and smoothly.

    Summary Rating:___

II. COMPETENCY AS A DECISION MAKER

Indicators: Planning, Assessment, Problem Solving, and Methods, Materials and Resources

Section II Evaluation: [   ]

Planning Indicators:

1. *Organizes a field notebook and maintains it throughout the internship.*
2. *Demonstrates long-range planning skills.*
3. *Plans well-developed lessons appropriate to the objectives.*
4. Plans instruction and activities appropriate to the students' academic levels, learning styles, and diverse perspectives (ethnic background, culture, community).
5. *Utilizes accurate and current content in lesson planning.*
6. Develops and/or uses curriculum that encourages students to question and interpret ideas.
7. Plans for the use of appropriate, available materials and technology to enhance lesson delivery. Demonstrates correct written expression in lesson plans.
8. *Submits daily lesson plans to cooperating teacher for approval at least one day prior to teaching.*
9. *Develops weekly schedule of plans and submits to university supervisor at the end of the week prior to teaching.*
10. *Develops a classroom management plan in accordance with policies of cooperating teacher and school.*

Summary Rating:____

Assessment Indicators:

1. Utilizes varied informal and formal assessment techniques to evaluate academic performance of students (e.g., observations, portfolios, teacher-made tests, performance tasks, student self-assessment, peer assessment, and diagnostic and standardized tests).
2. Uses evaluative feedback from student performance and adjusts instruction accordingly.
3. Helps students become aware of their strengths and growth needs by involving them in self-assessment activities.
4. Solicits information about students' experiences, learning behaviors, needs, and progress from parents, colleagues, and students themselves.
5. Incorporates technology in evaluating/assessing students' performance.
6. Prepares tests and assessments to determine learner progress, interests, and performance levels.

7. *Grades, records, and returns students' work in a timely manner.*
8. Uses records and students' work samples to support assessment and grading reports to parents.
9. *Determines grades and students' progress in keeping with school policies and procedures.*

   Summary Rating:____

Problem-Solving Indicators:

1. Uses varied decision-making approaches and critical-thinking skills when responding to problematic situations.
2. Utilizes a variety of approaches in order to promote decision making and development of critical-thinking skills in the classroom.
3. Provides opportunities for students to solve problems, make decisions, and express understanding of concepts, skills, and behaviors.
4. Designs opportunities for students to acquire knowledge and test hypotheses.
5. Shows objectivity when dealing with problems.

   Summary Rating:____

Methods, Materials, and Resources Indicators:

1. *Demonstrates a working repertoire of instructional strategies, approaches, or models.*
2. Takes materials and resources and his/her knowledge of instructional methods into account when planning instruction.
3. *Produces, creates, and utilizes unique instructional materials and resources from information sources and available technology.*

   Summary Rating:____

III. COMPETENCY AS A LEADER

Indicators: Leadership, Reflection and Metacognition, Ethical Perspectives, Research and Evaluation

Section III Evaluation:

Leadership Indicators:

1. Demonstrates initiative for assuming responsibility.
2. Effectively uses time at school.
3. Responds professionally to crisis situations.
4. Demonstrates enthusiasm for teaching and working with others.

5. Exhibits a positive attitude toward the profession.
6. Works well with colleagues.

   Summary Rating:____

Reflection and Metacognition Indicators:

1. *Documents self-evaluation and reflection on the extent to which stated objectives have been met for each lesson taught.*
2. *Reflects critically on teaching performance through written critiques of videotaped sessions.*
3. *Maintains a journal of reflection (addressing specifically the affective domain of the teaching experience).*
4. *Articulates the ability to be a reflective teacher (capable of adjusting and regulating teacher behaviors) as evidenced through Weekly Conference Reports and conferences with the cooperating teacher and college supervisor.*
5. Accepts and utilizes evaluative feedback to change the environment and/or teaching behaviors to improve performance.

   Summary Rating:____

Ethical Perspectives Indicators:

1. *Fulfills attendance requirements and maintains hours set by the school.*
2. *Attends professional and school-related meetings.*
3. *Attends university seminars as required.*
4. Dresses appropriately
5. Respects confidentiality of students and teachers.
6. Demonstrates working knowledge of school policies and procedures.
7. Adheres to the Standards of Conduct set forth in the Code of Ethics for the teaching profession in the state of Georgia.

   Summary Rating:____

Research and Evaluation Indicators:

1. Reflects on and evaluates teaching and learning for the purpose of revising practice.
2. Utilizes resources available for professional learning (i.e., professional literature, colleagues, associations, and professional development activities).
3. Applies in the classroom knowledge of educational research on teaching and learning.
4. *Uses experiences and resources to produce and maintain a professional portfolio.*

   Summary Rating:_____

APPENDIX B
MENTOR TEACHER PREFERENCE CHECKLIST

Dear Mentee:

As part of our effort to facilitate the best match between the mentee and the mentor, please complete the *Mentor Teacher Preference Checklist*. Be assured that your responses will be used only to provide direction in recommending the teams for our Teacher-Mentoring Program. Read the preference factor and then identify how important this issue is to you in making the best match.

1. Least important
2. Somewhat important
3. Undecided
4. Important
5. Very Important

Mentee Name: _____ **Subject Area:** _____ **Grade:** _____

Preference Factors	1	2	3	4	5
• I prefer to have a mentor who teaches the same subject.					
• I prefer to have a mentor who teaches the same grade level.					
• I prefer to have a mentor who is located near my classroom, shares a common planning time, and/or lunch period.					
• I prefer to have a mentor who is the same gender as myself.					
• I prefer to have a mentor who is about my age. 21–30___ 30–40___ 40–50___ 50+___					
• I prefer a mentor who is particularly skilled in the following areas:					
• I prefer …					

Comments, Questions, or Concerns:

APPENDIX C
MENTORING AGENDA FOR COOPERATING TEACHERS

What follows is a suggested agenda to provide a framework to guide your mentoring tasks. This outline is not a mandate that is designed to force you into a predetermined format; rather, it is a sketch to guide your efforts as you attempt to help a novice learn a wide range of new skills.

PRIOR TO THE FIELD EXPERIENCE

1. Set up an informal interview with intern.
2. Use Competency 2.1, "Cooperating Teacher-Mentor Interview Guide" (p. 54), to develop your interview questions.
3. Prepare an information packet of school-related materials.
4. Give a short guided tour of school.
5. Introduce intern to team members via a coffee or lunch.

BEGINNING OF FIELD EXPERIENCE

1. Develop your mentoring plan
   - Assess needs of the intern using Competency 2.6, "Needs Assessment for Beginning Teachers" (p. 69), as a way to identify intern's concerns.
   - Develop a priority list of needs to help intern set performance goals and objectives.
   - Use Competency 2.3, "Planning Guide" (p. 58), as away to focus intern on targeted goals.
   - Confirm tasks that need to be completed during the field experience. Ask for any guidelines and assessment forms that the teacher preparation requires/requests.
   - Assist the intern in developing a projected timeline to accomplish and monitor these tasks.
2. Establish a systematic performance-coaching schedule using the five-step process outlined in Competency 4, "Developing Your Performance-Coaching Skills." Here's a sample outline:

Mentor Tasks	*Week 1*	*Week 2*	*Week 3*	*Week 4*	*Week 5*
Step 1: Presenting/Clarifying Information via • Interviews • Weekly chats • Conferences • Team planning • E-mail • Telephone contacts	Day: Time: Place:				
Step 2: Demonstrating /Modeling Specific Teaching and Classroom Management Behaviors via • Classroom demonstration • Co-teaching • Seminars/workshops • Teaching videos	Day: Time: Place:				
Step 3: Observe Intern Practice of Modeled Behaviors via • Follow-up teaching • Group work with students • Co-teaching • Managing students during noninstructional duties (e.g., homeroom, locker breaks, lunch, library visits, after-school activities, etc.)	Day: Time: Place:				
Step 4: Coaching Sessions via • Observation forms • Videotaped lesson review • Verbal cues/reminders/tips • Informal chats • Formal pre- and postconferences in the clinical coaching cycle.	Day: Time: Place:				
Step 5: Reflection on Mentoring Process via • Assessment forms • Informal chats • Formal conferences • Program evaluation • Meetings with supervisors	Day: Time: Place:				

PREPARING INTERN TO TEACH AND MANAGE STUDENTS

1. Review your classroom rules and expectations using Competency 6.1, "Classroom Management Conference" (p. 133), as a guide.

2. Discuss appropriate teacher-student relationships (see Competency 6 for suggestions).

3. Discuss and clarify the standards for effective teaching that you will use to guide your feedback. See Competency 5.1, "Reflection Guide for Curriculum Planning" (p. 116), for possible suggestions.

4. Clarify and review any diversity issues (see Competency 7 for suggested tips).

5. Review the five stages of the coaching cycle—Preobservation Conference, Observation and Data Collection, Analysis and Strategy, Postobservation Conference, and Coaching Cycle Reflection— and the ways you will collect data about the intern's performance. (See Competency 4 for a complete summary.)

COACHING PERFORMANCE

1. Implement the five stages of the coaching cycle.
2. Review targeted goals and objectives and revise as needed.
3. Assist the intern in clearly identifying strengths and growth targets.

REFLECTING ON YOUR MENTORING SKILLS

1. Assess yourself and then ask the intern to give you feedback on your mentoring skills using Competency 1.2, "Mentor Teacher Evaluation" (p. 46).

APPENDIX D
AGENDA FOR FIRST-YEAR TEACHER MENTORS

What follows is a suggested agenda to provide a framework to guide your mentoring tasks. This outline is not a mandate that is designed to force you into a predetermined format; rather, it is a sketch to guide your efforts as you attempt to help entry-level teachers learn a wide range of new skills.

Not all topics listed here are addressed in this text, but information should be available to you through your school or district. Where possible we have directed you to a specific competency module for information or suggested resources.

PRIOR TO THE OPENING OF SCHOOL

1. Set up an informal interview with new teacher.
2. Use Competency 2.2, "First-Year Peer-Mentor Interview Guide" (p. 55), to develop your interview questions
3. Prepare an information packet of school-related materials.
4. Introduce new teacher to team members via a coffee or lunch.

DURING PREPLANNING

1. Discuss the planning for the first two weeks of school. Use Competency 6.2, "Reflection Dialogue Conference" (p. 135), and Competency 6.3, "Classroom Management Survival Checklist" (p. 136), as way to guide your discussion.
2. Develop your mentoring plan.
   - Assess needs of new teacher using Competency 2.6, "Needs Assessment for Beginning Teachers" (p. 69), as a way to identify concerns.
   - Develop a priority list of needs to help set performance goals and objectives.
   - Use Competency 2.3, "Planning Guide" (p. 58), as away to focus novice on targeted goals.
   - Assist the new teacher in developing a projected timeline to accomplish and monitor these goals.
3. Establish a systematic performance-coaching schedule using the five-step process outlined in Competency 4, "Developing Your Performance-Coaching Skills." Here's a sample outline:

Mentor Tasks	Week 1	Week 2	Week 3	Week 4	Week 5
Step 1: Presenting/Clarifying Information via • Interviews • Daily/weekly chats • Conferences • Team planning meetings • E-mail contacts • Telephone contacts • Professional meetings/conferences	Day: Time: Place:				
Step 2: Demonstrating/Modeling Specific Teaching and Classroom Management Behaviors via • Classroom demonstrations • Peer visitations • Co-teaching • Parent conferences • Seminars/workshops • Teaching videos • Staff development workshops	Day: Time: Place:				
Step 3: Observing Novice Practice of Modeled Behaviors via • Teaching • Co-teaching/team teaching • Managing students during extracurricular activities	Day: Time: Place:				
Step 4: Coaching Sessions via • Observation forms • Videotaped lesson review • Verbal cues/reminders/tips • Informal chats • Formal pre- and postobservation conferences in the clinical coaching cycle	Day: Time: Place:				
Step 5: Reflection on Mentoring Process via • Assessment forms • Informal chats • Formal conferences • Program evaluations • Meetings with supervisors	Day: Time: Place:				

COACHING CYCLE FOCUS

What follows is a suggested topic outline of instructional skills new teachers need to know about and develop. The timeline for each coaching cycle will depend upon the knowledge and skill level of the individual new teacher. We suggest that you divide the school year into four parts and use this as a way to guide the professional development of the first-year teacher. Each cycle could be planned using the five-step coaching schedule presented above.

- ◆ First Coaching Cycle
  - Preparing Effective Lessons (see Competency 5)
  - Managing Student Behavior (see Competency 6)
  - Communicating with Parents
- ◆ Second Coaching Cycle
  - Conferencing Skills with Parents
  - Identifying Students with Special Needs
  - Structuring the Class to Meet Individual Student Differences (see Competency 7)
  - Developing Questioning Strategies (see Competency 5)
- ◆ Third Coaching Cycle
  - Oral and Written Communication Skills
  - Presentation Skills and Body Language
  - Lesson Development and Transitions (see Competency 5)
  - Student Assessment and Evaluation (see Competency 5)
  - Conferencing Skills with Students
- ◆ Fourth Coaching Cycle
  - Developing Lessons to Meet Individual Learning Styles (see Competency 5)
  - Assessment of Social Insight and With-it-ness (see Competency 7)
  - Problem-Solving Techniques and Use of Conflict Resolution Skills (see Competency 2)
  - Teaching Flexibility and Adaptability (see Competency 8)
  - Professional Duties and Responsibilities (see Competency 8)
  - Integration of Technology and Learning (see Competency 5)

POSTPLANNING

1. Reflection on Teaching Performance Standards (see Competency 5)
2. Reflection on Classroom Management Standards (see Competency 6)
3. Reflection on Professional Responsibility Standards (see Competency 8)
4. Reflection on Mentoring Program (see Competency 1)
   - Assess yourself and then ask the intern to give you feedback on your mentoring skills using Competency 1.2, "Mentor Teacher Evaluation" (p. 46).

APPENDIX E
FIRST-YEAR TEACHER CHECKLIST AND REMINDERS

To help with planning here's a checklist you might review, modify, and share with your mentee to help with the first six to nine weeks of school.

PRE-PLANNING

Instructional Planning	
	• Review curriculum guides and general course syllabi
	• Obtain teacher's edition of textbooks
	• Identify the major areas to teach for the first four to six weeks
	• Look at the school calendar for the first six weeks. Develop a timeline of topics and skills for this time frame. Match your outline to the mandated allotment of time required for each subject.
	• Prepare a topic outline for the year.
Organizational Policies and Procedures	
	• Review school policies and student handbooks. Specifically check: Bus duty Student registration procedures Homework policy Field trips Dress code Emergency procedures (tornado, fire drills, injuries, etc.)
	• Review school district policies/faculty handbook. Specifically check: Sick/personal leave procedures Conduct code Crisis plan Attendance Substitute procurement Professional insurance
	• Review the school goals and/or school improvement plans.

	• Find out about the school culture as it relates to:
	    Induction orientation activities
	    Staff development programs
	    Teacher mentoring options
	    Emphasis on professional development
	    Reassignment and transfer procedures
	    Supervision and evaluation
	    Contracts, regulations, and waivers

Classroom Organization	

	• Think about the first week of school and design the physical layout:
	    Large group arrangement
	    Small group areas
	    Bulletin boards
	    Quiet/time-out area
	    Position of your desk
	    Organization of materials and supplies
	    Filing system
	    Traffic flow
	    Seating arrangement and seating charts

	• Plan how to handle/record daily routines and student interactions:
	    Entering the room
	    Assigning seats
	    Lunch money and charges
	    Receipt books
	    Grade books
	    Attendance records
	    Absentees excuses
	    Plan book
	    Textbook distribution

	• Plan how to manage student behavior:
	    Establishing class rules and procedures
	    Enforcing rules and consequences fairly
	    Teaching class rules and procedures
	    Helping students to monitor own behavior and self-correct
	    Minimizing transitions between learning tasks
	    Establishing a businesslike climate
	    Setting reasonable expectations

First 6–9 Weeks

Instructional Preparation	
	• Assess lesson plans: Teacher directed, motivating, successful for all students Directions are easy to follow and not overly complicated Students work more as a large group until teacher knows students and classroom management procedures are routine
	• Size up activities, projects, groups and learning centers: Planned in advance and match learning objectives Procedures and sequence of events are clearly described Resources and materials ordered/prepared well ahead.
	• Develop substitute teacher plans: Includes the daily schedule for each class Includes the seating roster for each class Identifies any student who might present a problem and a plan to correct Lesson plans are detailed and all materials are duplicated, ready for distribution, and easily found in your room Classroom rules and procedures are outlined
	• Think about supervision and evaluation: Review the school evaluation form Ask for a preliminary assessment before the official one to get sense of evaluator's supervisory style and school focus for teaching
Managing Individuals Differences	
	• Identify student needs and interests: As a class As individuals
	• Assess and evaluate students by: Recording daily grades Observing students Varying the type of assessment (cognitive, affective, psychomotor) Placement of students

	• Assign students to groups: Devising procedures for group work Communicating expectations to group members including roles and assignments Finding out about cooperative learning and how groups function
	• Develop modified education plans for special needs students
	• Design alternative lessons and activities for students with special needs
	• Formulate homework policy: Amount and frequency Weight and impact on course grade Coordination with team or department
Implementing Classroom Management Plan	
	• Establish rules and procedures and post
	• Reinforce positive behavior routinely
	• Enforce of rules and procedures consistently
	• Document student behavior is systematically
	• Design a classroom management plan and share with peers and administrative team
Home-School Communications	
	• Orient parents at night meeting: Handout on course syllabi and grading procedures Student expectations How parents can help

	• Develop personal communication skills:
	   Oral Expression
	      Voice tone and modulation
	      Correct grammar and mechanics
	      Clear directions
	   Written Expression
	      Correct grammar and mechanics
	      Clear and concise writing
	      Professional yet inviting tone

	• Develop ways to get students' work home
	• Develop a descriptive rather than a judgmental communication style when communicating with students, parents, and peers

	• Prepare report cards/evaluations for students:
	   Filling in information accurately
	   Marking attendance
	   Determining grades
	   Reporting student conduct
	   Checking for signatures and conferences requests

	• Monitoring professional development by:
	   Observing/modeling a peer teacher
	   Videotaping your lessons and assessing your performance
	   Attending staff-development workshops
	   Seeking feedback from a peer
	   Preparing for your first official evaluation

APPENDIX F
CRITERIA FOR UNIT PLAN EVALUATION

Rating Scale:

5 = Outstanding: All indicators addressed thoroughly and with detail.

4 = Very Good: Most indicators addressed thoroughly and with sufficient detail.

3 = Satisfactory: All or most indicators addressed but detail is moderate.

2 = Needs Improvement: Indicators are not addressed in more than one component and/or detail is less than moderate or does not support the component.

1 = Unacceptable: Components and indicators are missing.

Unit Components and Indicators	*Rating and Comments* 5-4-3-2-1
Group Description 1. Grade level and subject 2. General academic achievement of group/class 3. General behavioral description of group/class 4. General description of class/group as it relates to gender, race, class, and cultural composition.	
Unit Rationale 1. Description of why and how you chose this unit 2. Explanation of how it fits into the curriculum 3. Projection of student interest in the unit and topic relevance to students	
Objectives 1. Stated as learner outcomes 2. Describe adequate amount/level of content 3. Appropriate to ability and group description as noted in unit plan 4. Reflect learning styles 5. Reflect application of state and national curriculum guides and content standards	

Unit Components and Indicators	*Rating and Comments* *5-4-3-2-1*
Content Outline 1. Content clearly detailed 2. Content sequenced logically 3. Balance of content is appropriate	
Instructional Plans 1. Plans reflect important components of effective lessons showing adequate planning by teacher during the initial development of content 2. Activities are appropriate for student abilities 3. Activities provide learners practice on objectives 4. Information presented is accurate and current 5. Instructional resources are appropriate for activities, objectives, and students 6. Materials supplement basic curriculum text 7. Opportunities are provided for students to process content through a variety of instructional strategies (skits, simulations, cooperative learning, and hands-on activities) 8. Plans alternate activities for students that show awareness of learner style, reading level, and ability level 9. Plans review and other follow-up activities to reinforce learning	
Assessment 1. Determines knowledge of content and or prerequisites through appropriate pre-test 2. Evaluates and describes pre-test results 3. Informal assessments are included as needed 4. Criteria or components of satisfactory performance are specified 5. At least one formative assessment which addresses objectives and provides recordable data on each student is included 6. Includes summative test items which elicit the behaviors specified (post-test) 7. Plans to elicit two or more types (i.e., performance, inquiry, essay, short answer) of responses from students during summative assessment 8. Assessment tools are coded to unit objectives	

Unit Components and Indicators	Rating and Comments 5-4-3-2-1
Communication 1. Unit plan reflects professionalism in organization and presentation 2. Writing intended for learners is legible and reflects use of technology if appropriate 3. Mechanics of English are correct 4. A bibliography of resources and references is included 5. Proper documentation of handouts/materials with daily lesson plans is evident	
Interdisciplinary Connections 1. Listing of suggested interdisciplinary topics is included 2. Related activities to other content areas are suggested 3. Linkage to multicultural/diversity topics and activities is included as indicated by the general group description	

Overall Unit Assessment: _____

Comments:

APPENDIX G
LESSON PLAN TEMPLATE

Lesson planning varies within content areas and across grade levels. The purpose of this sample is to help interns and first-year teachers develop lessons based on the elements of effective instruction. We encourage you to review this example and modify it to meet your needs.

Lesson Title: _____ **Level:** _____

Teacher: _____ **Date:** _____

State or National Content Standards	*Lesson Input— Step-by-Step Procedures*
	Instructional strategies to consider to meet your objectives: lecture, discussion, textbook, recitation, cooperative learning, discovery, role play, peer tutoring, problem-solving, oral and written work, drill and practice, computer-assisted instruction, simulation, guided practice, independent work.
Performance Objectives Student will: Objective #1 Objective #2 Objective #3	**Beginning the Lesson** Gain attention Focus on objective Relate to students' experiences
Student Evaluation Objective #1 Objective #2 Objective #3	**Middle of the Lesson** (Describe in detail your lesson sequence and teaching strategies. Number each step. Include how you will check for understanding.)

| *Materials Needed* | **Middle of Lesson** (*continued*) |
| | **End of Lesson**
(Summary, follow-up activities, homework) |

Supplemental Materials—Extension Activities—Backup Plan

Classroom Management Strategies for This Lesson

APPENDIX H
CLASSROOM MANAGEMENT PLAN TEMPLATE

First-year teachers confront multiple tasks simultaneously. Mentor teachers may need to assist novices in thinking ahead on issues related to running a smoothly operated classroom. Here is a brief outline to trigger their thoughts and guide their actions during the critical first weeks.

A. Developing a Business-like Classroom	B. Articulating Your Philosophy	C. Clarifying Your Expectations
Describe your desired interactions with students. Focus on the climate you want to establish. Describe intended students' interactions with one another. Focus on how you want students to treat one another. Identify the methods you will use to achieve these interactions.	What beliefs do you hold about: • Teaching and learning? • Managing students?	What are your classroom rules? List them here: What are the consequences? How are these rules and consequences communicated to students? How are students recognized for following the rules? How will you monitor and keep records of student behavior?
D. Knowing School Policy	**E. Designing Your Classroom**	**F. Establishing Procedures**
Review the following if they are available: Jot down the key information you need to know. • Student Handbook • Teacher Handbook • Substitute Handbook • Emergency Procedures • Security Procedures	Describe your classroom and how you will arrange it. Direct comments about: • Bulletin boards • Quiet areas • Filing system • Traffic flow • Seating arrangements	How will you settle the students and get them ready for learning tasks? What procedures have you developed for taking roll, collecting papers, working in groups, and any other noninstructional responsibility? How will you handle transitions between learning segments?
G. Referring Students	**H. Sizing Up Your Classes**	**I. Targeting Effective Lessons**
What are the procedures for referring/sending a student to the office? What are the procedures if you suspect child abuse? What services are offered through the school for guidance and counseling of students?	Describe the general composition of your classes as it relates to: • Gender • Behavior • Ethnic/Cultural Composition • Special Needs What modifications/approaches are needed for each class if any?	What lessons have you planned for the first weeks of school? Are they of high interest to students and easy to implement? What backup plans need to be in place in case of unexpected school drills/emergencies or your absence?

APPENDIX I
DAILY REFLECTION GUIDE

Name: _____ Date: _____

Respond to these questions in three to five sentences.

As a Facilitator of Learning Refer to one or more of these areas— *Subject Matter Knowledge, Individual Differences, Classroom Management*	*As a Decision Maker* Refer to one or more these areas— *Planning, Assessing, Problem Solving, and Methods and Materials*
What activities I did today?	**What activities I did today?**
What I learned today?	**What I learned today?**
Lesson Evaluation if I taught today or Critique of Lesson I observed today.	**Classroom Management Skills I practiced today.**